OFFICIALLY NOTED

IN PROFILE

Explorers on the Nile

Andrew Langley

SILVER BURDETT

In Profile

Women of the Air
Founders of Religions
Tyrants of the Twentieth Century
Leaders of the Russian Revolution
Pirates and Privateers
Great Press Barons
Explorers on the Nile
Women Prime Ministers
The Founders of America
The Cinema Greats
The War Poets
The First Men Round the World

First published in 1981 by
Wayland Publishers Ltd
49 Lansdowne Place, Hove
East Sussex BN3 1HF, England

© Copyright 1981 Wayland Publishers Ltd

Adapted and Published in the United States by
Silver Burdett Company, Morristown, N.J.

1982 Printing

ISBN 0-382-06637-5

Library of Congress Catalog Card No. 81-86275

Phototypeset by Direct Image, Hove, Sussex
Printed in the U.K. by Cripplegate Printing Co. Ltd.

Contents

John Hanning Speke — 5
Speke discovers Lake Victoria — 8
The outlet from Lake Victoria is found — 12
Burton attacks Speke's discovery — 16
Dates and events — 17

Sir Samuel Baker — 19
Down the Nile to Gondokoro — 22
Lake Albert: source of the Nile? — 25
Baker conquers the Nile basin — 28
Dates and events — 31

David Livingstone — 33
The first Englishman to cross Africa — 35
The Zambesi expedition fails — 39
The fatal quest for the source of the Nile — 42
Dates and events — 47

Henry Morton Stanley — 49
Stanley finds Livingstone in Ujiji — 52
The Nile question is finally settled — 54
Stanley's expedition to rescue Emin Pasha — 58
Dates and events — 61

Glossary — 62
Further reading — 62
Index — 63

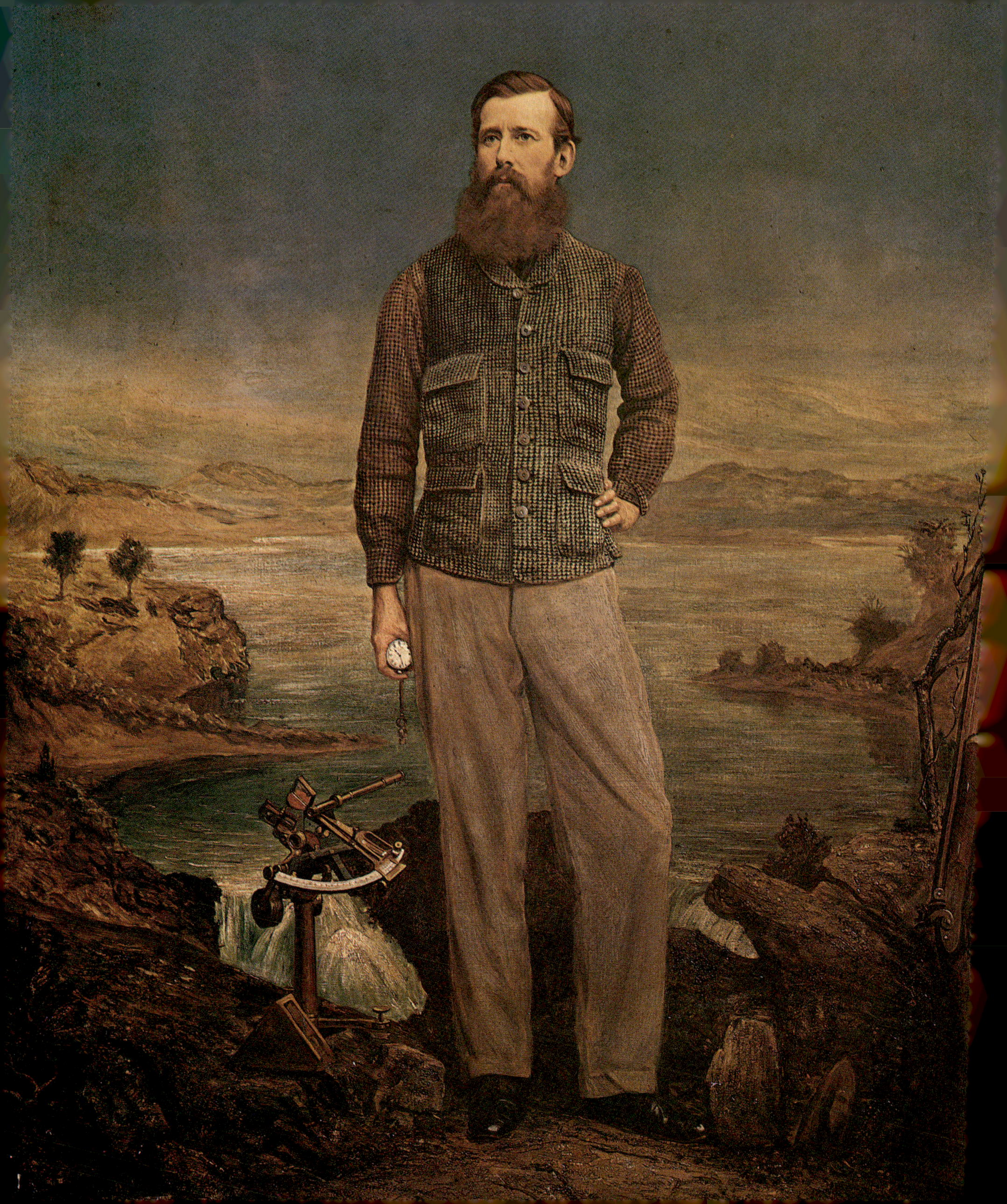

John Hanning Speke

The source of the mighty River Nile remained a mystery for centuries. Then, in 1862, John Hanning Speke discovered Lake Victoria. On his return to England, many refused to believe his claim that this was where the river rose. Tragically, he died in a shooting accident before he could prove his case. But later explorers justified his claims and today he is remembered as the most important of all the explorers of the Nile.

From an early age, it was clear that John Hanning Speke—'Jack' to his friends—was going to be an adventurer. With his easy-going parents, and his six brothers and sisters, he lived a happy country life in the security of Orleigh Court, near the North Devon coast. He was sent to school first in nearby Barnstaple and then in faraway Blackheath, but he never cared much for lessons. He was too busy out in the fields hunting rabbits, or dreaming of shooting big game in Africa.

The army was the obvious career for him, and his mother, a friend of the Duke of Wellington, was able to secure him a commission in a regiment in India. In 1844, at the age of only seventeen, Speke sailed out to the Punjab in search of glamorous adventures. He was soon disappointed by the strictness of army life, even though he fought in several bloody battles in the Punjab War and in the war against the Sikhs.

In 1849 he made the most important decision of his life. He planned a long trip into the centre of Africa, shooting, mapping and exploring in what was then almost unknown territory. To do this, he had to get extended leave from his regiment, and save up as much as he could for equipment and travel. He prepared himself by spending every spare moment hunting in the Himalayas and Tibet.

This portrait of Richard Burton was painted when he was thirty-nine years old.

By the time Speke took the boat from Bombay to Aden, he had grown up into a tall but wiry young man, fit, strong and determined enough for any hardship. Although he did not make friends easily, preferring to travel alone and to run his own affairs, his blue eyes, fair hair and striking physique impressed anyone he met.

He certainly impressed Richard Burton when they met in 1854. Burton was by then a famous traveller and one of the first white men to have entered the

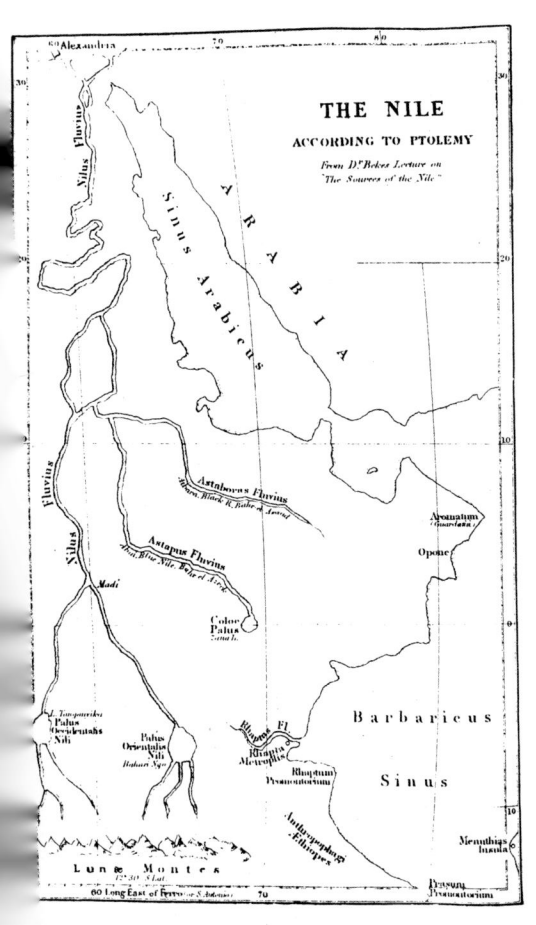

Ptolemy's map of the Nile showing the river flowing out of a range of mountains called Lunae Montes, *or Mountains of the Moon.*

holy Islamic cities of Mecca and Harar, where discovery would have meant certain death. Now he was planning an expedition through Somalia and Ethiopia to Zanzibar, and from there west across Africa to the Atlantic. His public purpose was to open up the continent for trade.

But Burton had private reasons as well. He had heard stories from Arab traders about huge lakes and snowcapped mountains that lay west of Zanzibar. Could the melting snow from these mountains, filling the lakes, be the true source of the river Nile?

The Nile's mystery

The Nile had always been one of the world's mysteries. Where it flowed into the Mediterranean sea, thousands of miles to the north of its source, near Cairo, it had once been worshipped as a god. It never failed, bringing fertility to a vast area of land. But it seemed to flow straight out of a desert. How could it do this without drying up? And where did all these tons of water come from?

The Egyptians, Greeks and Romans had all tried to find the source, but failed. The famous geographer, Ptolemy, drew his map of the world in about A.D. 150, and it showed the river flowing out of a range called the Mountains of the Moon. He based this on the story of a Greek merchant who had travelled in that area.

These mountains remained a riddle for many years. Although a Scotsman called James Bruce traced the source of the main tributary—called the Blue Nile—no one managed to follow the course of the main river—the White Nile—farther south than latitude 5°N. Burton hoped that by approaching the lakes from the east (a much shorter distance), he could settle the mystery once and for all.

Speke discovers Lake Victoria

Burton invites Speke to join his expedition ... Burton and Speke are wounded ... Speke recovers and returns home ... He joins Burton's second expedition ... Lake Tanganyika is not the Nile's source ... Speke leaves Burton and discovers Lake Victoria ... Burton disbelieves him ... Speke steals the limelight in England ... Organizes a second trip to Lake Victoria.

Until Speke met Burton, it seemed as though all his dreams would be shattered. The British Resident in Aden considered his expedition much too dangerous and refused to give him letters of introduction to the tribal chiefs which might have assured his safe passage. Burton's party, on the other hand, was backed by the Royal Geographical Society in London.

So, when Burton offered Speke a place on his expedition, he jumped at the chance. The whole enterprise, however, was doomed to disaster. Speke's first job was to lead a small party into central Somalia, to explore and to collect camels and ponies for transport. Knowing little of the customs or of the language, he was soon in danger of his life—not only from the savage tribesmen of the interior, but also from his own porters.

Somehow he managed to get back to Aden, but much worse was to follow. Burton's small force had not even set out from the coast when they were attacked at night by local tribesmen, and both he and Speke were wounded in the fighting: Speke being stabbed in the shoulder, chest and thighs.

Speke escaping from hostile Somalian tribesmen with his hands still bound together by a rope.

A battlescene from the Crimean War. Speke volunteered for the campaign after his Somaliland adventure.

They sailed back to Aden, where Speke made a miraculous recovery, and then returned to England. But Speke had more to suffer. Not only was the expedition criticized by the British Government, but he had lost all his valuable equipment, plundered by the Somalians. On top of all this, Burton wrote a bestseller about the trip, which included extracts from Speke's own diary.

Putting aside his African plans, Speke rejoined the army during the closing stages of the Crimean War. He still dreamed of exploring the Nile, so when Burton later invited him to join a second expedition, he was overjoyed. After obtaining further leave from his regiment, and collecting a new set of equipment, he set sail for Zanzibar.

In 1857, the party of nearly 150 men set out from the east coast near the island of Zanzibar, heading for Lake Tanganyika. Progress was very slow and all around them they saw the shocking evidence of the slave trade, passing huge caravans of prisoners, and

A view of Zanzibar's sea front. The island lies just off the east coast of Africa.

finding many abandoned corpses.

As the journey progressed, Burton and Speke were struck down with fever and were nearly blinded by eye diseases. After an agonizing seven-month trek, they reached the shores of Lake Tanganyika. No white man had ever been there before, and Burton was sure that it was the source of the Nile. But he was soon proved wrong. They found a river at the northern end of the lake which flowed *into* it rather than out of it, and could not possibly be the Nile. This depressing news, on top of the fact that their supplies were running low, made Burton anxious to return.

Lake Victoria's discovery

As he was still very ill, they stopped to rest on the way back. Speke took advantage of the halt to see if he could find a legendary lake which the Africans called 'Nyanza', some distance to the north. It was a fateful decision. After a three-week march, Speke glimpsed a vast sheet of water, much bigger even than Lake Tanganyika. He named it Lake Victoria, in honour of the Queen. In a moment of inspiration,

Lake Victoria, the largest lake in Africa, was discovered by Speke in 1858.

Speke guessed that here was the true beginning of the Nile. He could not prove it, of course, because the Nile would flow out of the northern end, while he was at the southern tip, 400 miles (640 km) away.

In years to come, his guess was to prove correct, in spite of the wrangling and tragedy that followed. Burton was angry at missing out on the discovery, and refused to believe Speke's theory. His jealousy in turn angered Speke, and their friendship slowly turned sour. The journey back to the coast was a miserable one. As well as arguing heatedly with his leader, Speke became delirious with fever.

Fame for Speke

Speke was the first to arrive back in England in 1859. He immediately told the President of the Royal Geographical Society, Sir Roderick Murchison, of his exciting discovery, and of his theory that Lake Victoria was the true source of the Nile. When Burton returned a few days later, he was enraged to find that Speke was a famous man, and that the original triumph of the expedition—the discovery of Lake Tanganyika— had been forgotten. Articles by Speke appeared in the press and he was invited to address the Royal Geographical Society. Finally, he was given a grant of £2,500 to organize a second trip to Lake Victoria.

Sir Roderick Murchison, three times President of the Royal Geographical Society.

The outlet from Lake Victoria is found

Speke was overjoyed to be in charge at last. By now he was obsessed with his search for the source of the Nile. He felt that, once the geography of central Africa had been worked out, the continent would be open to all the benefits of European civilization—an end to the slave trade, conversion to Christianity, and a flood of Western goods.

There was no question of asking Richard Burton to join him. Speke's pride had been badly hurt by his companion's refusal to recognize his discovery, and he rather lost his head, accusing Burton of all sorts of crimes. Burton quietly set about gathering evidence to prove that Speke's inspired theory was wrong. The pair were not to meet again for five years.

Speke turned instead to James Grant, an old army friend. Grant was the perfect second-in-command for

Map showing the route that Speke and Grant took on their journey to find the source of the Nile.

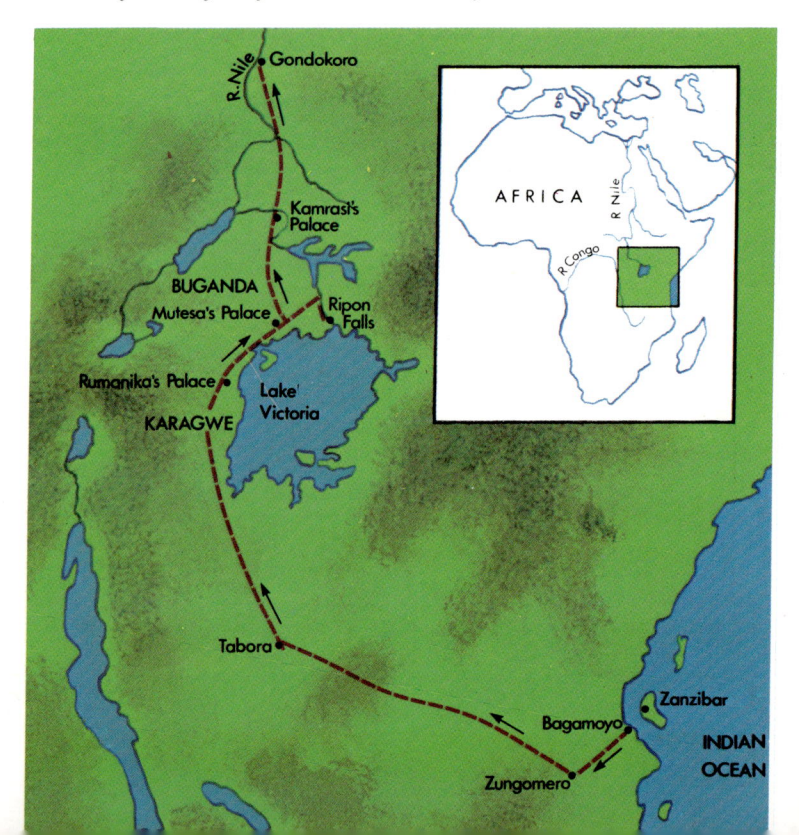

Burton and Speke still enemies... Takes Grant with him to Lake Victoria... They plan to find its northerly outlet... King Rumanika welcomes the expedition... Then they stay with fearsome King Mutesa... He is won over with gifts... He reluctantly lets them go... Grant goes to meet King Kamrasi... Speke discovers a waterfall from Lake Victoria and names it Ripon Falls.

James Grant, the man that accompanied Speke on his expedition to find the Nile's source.

the headstrong Speke, being a modest, trustworthy man who could be relied on never to make a fuss, and never to question his leader.

The aim of this new expedition was bold and simple. The party would travel north-west from the same point on the east coast where Burton and Speke had set out in 1857. On reaching Lake Victoria, they would continue round its edge until a northerly outlet was found. They would then simply follow this river northwards and, assuming that it really was the Nile, would eventually reach the town of Gondokoro. Here they would join up with a relief column led by John Petherick, who would travel down the river from Cairo. So, late in 1860, Speke and Grant sailed from Portsmouth to Zanzibar to prove conclusively that Speke's inspired theory was correct.

To begin with, Speke took much the same route as he had followed with Burton. Once again the progress was very slow. An enormous number of porters ran away, goats and cattle were stolen, and all but one of the pack mules died. The food also disappeared at a great rate, and Speke's skill with the rifle was often needed to fill the pot.

Grant was forced to travel on this litter because his leg was swollen.

Rubaga, the capital of the widely-feared King Mutesa.

After more than a year's marching, the party reached Karagwe, 600 miles (960 km) from the coast. This kingdom, on the western side of Lake Victoria, was ruled by Rumanika, an enlightened and friendly man, who made the travellers welcome.

But, pleasant though Karagwe was, Speke had to push on north to the land of Buganda, ruled by the savage and widely-feared King Mutesa. Unfortunately, Grant had a swollen leg, and was forced to lag behind. Speke arrived at Mutesa's court early in 1862, having had just one glimpse of Lake Victoria, way over to his right.

The meeting with Mutesa was a tricky moment for Speke. The king was fond of condemning people to death for little or no reason. Shortly before the explorer's arrival, he had ordered the execution of 450 men on the spur of the moment. But he was soon impressed with the forthright Speke, who had brought him many gifts—a gold watch, cloth, beads, a telescope and some guns. Mutesa was thrilled to see Speke's demonstration of what a rifle could do—so thrilled that he immediately handed the rifle to his page, with the instruction to go out and shoot someone. The order was obeyed without question.

The Ripon Falls

Speke spent nearly five months at Mutesa's court, during which time Grant arrived. The king was reluctant to let them go, but eventually the party set off north again. By now, Speke could not contain his curiosity about Lake Victoria, so he decided to march at great speed to where he thought the Nile would emerge. Grant, still suffering from the swelling in his leg, took the rest of the expedition on into the Bunyoro district, which was ruled by King Kamrasi.

Speke's small party soon struck the Nile. Travelling upstream along its banks, they eventually found the outlet from Lake Victoria. This was over a thundering waterfall, which Speke named the Ripon Falls (after a patron of the Royal Geographical Society). As he stood listening to the roar of the waters, it seemed to Speke that his expedition had found its goal.

The Ripon Falls from a drawing by Speke.

Burton attacks Speke's discovery

Hostile tribes prevent the exploration of Lake Victoria... Speke and Grant meet the Bakers at Gondokoro... Returns in triumph to London... Publishes two bestselling books... Burton attacks the expedition's findings... A debate between Speke and Burton is planned... Speke accidentally shoots himself before the meeting... His theory proved correct eleven years later.

Although he had now achieved his ambition, Speke was still a long way from home. Hostile natives prevented him from exploring Lake Victoria any farther, so he hurried to rejoin Grant. The friendly King Kamrasi lent the party canoes, in which they travelled down the Nile for a short way, glad of the rest from marching—Speke had walked every step of the way. But soon they were back on their feet, tramping through the scrubland towards Gondokoro and their relief supplies.

But when the twenty-two survivors arrived, exhausted and starved, some months later, they found, not Petherick, but Samuel Baker and his wife. Speke was furious with Petherick (unfairly) and was glad to accept food and supplies from the cheerful Baker. His main concern was to get quickly back to London, but he was pleased to hear, in Khartoum, that he had been awarded the Royal Geographical Society's Gold Medal.

His return was a triumph. He was given a reception by the Society in Piccadilly, where he made a speech, and the excited crowd broke several windows to hear him. He received congratulations from Queen Victoria and the Prince of Wales, and published two bestselling books, the *Journal* and *What Led to the Discovery of the Source of the Nile*.

But his enemies were soon hard at work. Burton, aided by a clever geographer called McQueen, began

Gondokoro, the then southernmost point of civilization on the Nile.

Speke and Grant's reception by the Royal Geographical Society on their return to London.

to find holes in Speke's arguments. He had not proved, they said, that the river which flowed over the Ripon Falls was in fact the Nile. They found fault with some of Speke's hastily taken measurements, which seemed to show that the river ran uphill! They even made uncomplimentary remarks about his behaviour among the natives.

In the summer of 1864, to clear the matter up, it was decided to hold a public debate in Bath between Speke and Burton. Poor Speke, a man of action who was not much of a public speaker, hated the thought of being stuck indoors. He longed to be back in the silence of the Himalayas. But he never took part in the debate. The day before it was due to take place, he went out shooting on the estate of a nearby cousin. Whilst clambering over a wall, he accidentally shot himself, and died soon afterwards.

Speke was never to see his theories about the Nile proved right. It was not until Stanley sailed right round Lake Victoria, eleven years later, that the world realized how harshly it had treated him.

Dates and events

1827 John Hanning Speke born in Ilminster, Devon.
1844 Joins the army in India and fights in the Punjab War.
1849 Obtains leave from the army to prepare himself for an expedition to Africa.
1854 Meets Richard Burton in Aden, and is invited to join his expedition.
1855 Tribesmen attack encampment of Burton and Speke in Somaliland.
1857 Second expedition with Burton, during which Speke discovers Lake Victoria.
1859 Returns to England and addresses the Royal Geographical Society.
1860 Leaves for Africa with Grant for a second trip to Lake Victoria.
1862 Arrives at King Mutesa's court. Reaches and names the Ripon Falls.
1863 Speke and Grant meet the Bakers at Gondokoro.
1864 Speke and Burton to debate the question of the Nile's source in Bath. Speke accidentally shoots himself (15th September).

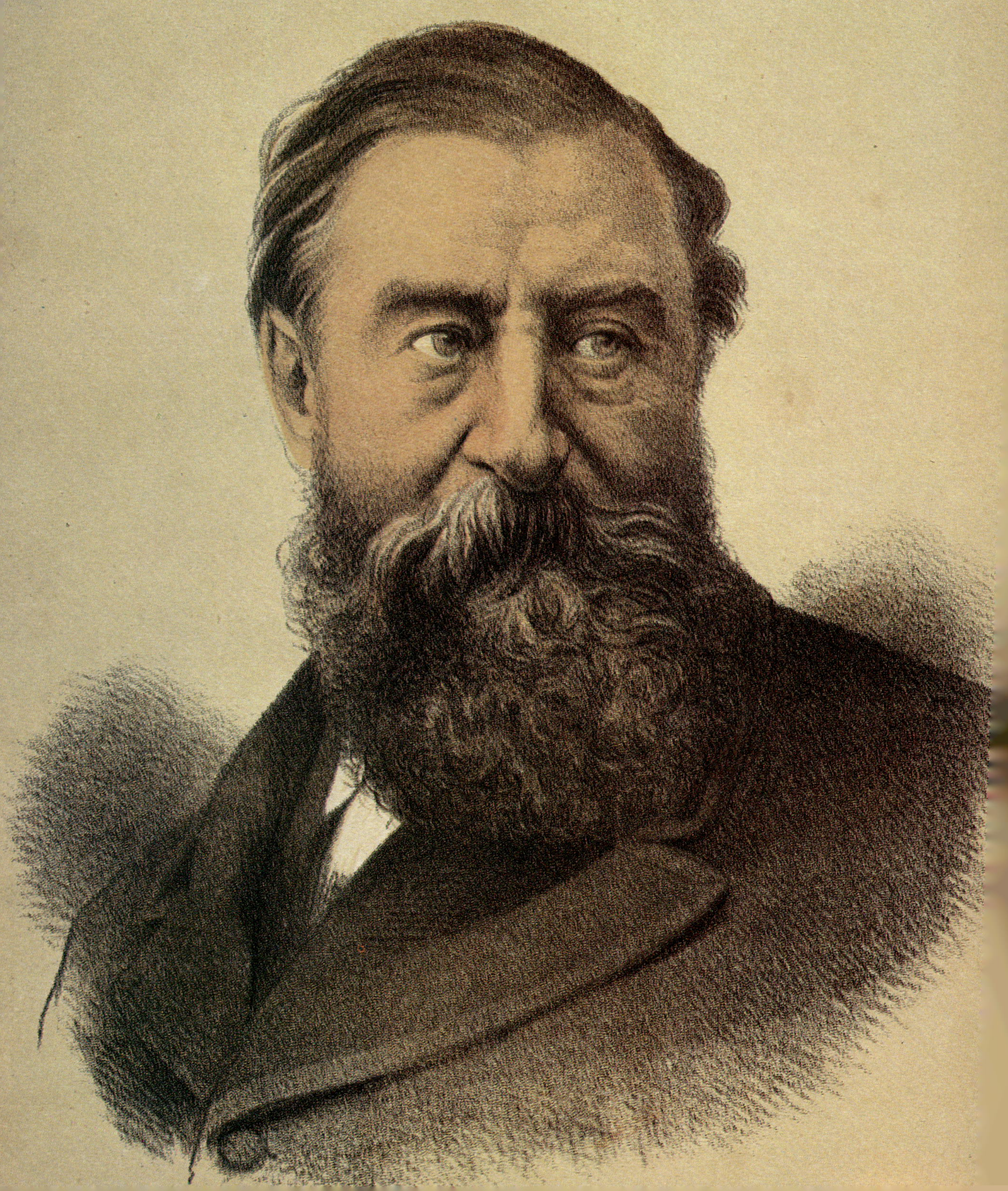

Sir Samuel Baker

Samuel Baker was a brave and tough traveller as well as a fearless hunter. He led an expedition to find the source of the Nile, and discovered Lake Albert and the Murchison Falls. He became a national hero and was knighted in 1866. Known throughout the Empire as 'Baker on the Nile', he returned to Africa and dealt a great blow to the slave trade by annexing the Nile basin around Gondokoro for the Egyptian government.

The young Sam Baker always hated school. Born in 1821, the second son of a successful merchant, he much preferred the outdoor life. Early on, he developed a passion for guns and hunting which lasted throughout his life. He even started making his own fireworks, though the first batch blew out the kitchen windows!

He was allowed to roam freely around the Gloucestershire countryside, rarely going to school. But in the end, his father decided that he must have some education, and sent him to a kindly tutor near London, where Sam enjoyed himself enormously. By now he was shooting mad. For a trip to Germany, he designed his own heavy-duty rifle, which weighed nearly 20 lb (10 kg), and needed a huge charge of gunpowder. It was a deadly weapon, and only a strong man could carry and fire it.

At the age of twenty-two he married his childhood sweetheart. Although he was never short of money, it was clear that he should settle down in his father's profitable sugar-plantation and shipping business. He started a desk job in London, but soon became bored. He persuaded his father to send him and his brother John out to Mauritius to manage one of the plantations. But life even on this exotic island was too dull for him. What he longed for was a wilder land, where he could hunt and explore to his heart's content, and push forward the frontiers of civilization. Soon, he found the very place he was looking for—Ceylon.

The Bakers left Mauritius in 1845, and eagerly began making plans to establish a settlement in Ceylon. Sam was sent out ahead, to explore the country and buy a suitable piece of land. Ceylon was then a beautiful and unspoilt island, famous for its crops of cinnamon and coffee.

When the rest of the family arrived, Sam had marked out and bought an estate in the hills. This had to be cleared of trees and fenced, and the fields had to be ploughed and sown. It was an arduous task, but the Bakers had brought with them a vast amount of equipment and stock, including a bull, a cow, sheep, sawmills, farming implements, horses and even a pack of foxhounds. Gradually they established themselves, and smart houses, a church and reading room were built.

Once the farm began to prosper, Sam was able to return to his first love, hunting. The countryside, with its forests, mountains, raging streams and teeming wildlife, was a paradise for him. He fished, and shot elephant and deer in great numbers, often

An early photograph of Kaduganawa Station, Ceylon.

Sam Baker shooting an enraged buffalo.

risking his life in his mad pursuit of big game. Once, when charged by an enraged buffalo, he found to his horror that he had no bullets left. Frantically, he tore a piece from his shirt, wrapped it round some coins in his pocket, and fired that, managing to stun the animal.

His greatest joy was to hunt stags, boars and leopards on foot with his hounds, armed with nothing but a hunting knife. He would spend whole days and nights in the wilds, racing to keep up with the dogs, swimming swollen rivers and scarcely having time to eat. Although it might seem that Sam Baker was simply enjoying himself, he was learning to survive, and toughening himself for the far harsher trials ahead.

After eight years, the Bakers caught the wanderlust again. Leaving the farm in charge of a bailiff, they returned to England. Sam was by now the proud father of four daughters, although three other children had died. As his wife was in poor health, weakened by the climate of Ceylon, he decided to avoid the English winter by taking her to the Pyrenees. But it was all in vain; she died of typhoid, leaving Sam heartbroken and homeless.

Down the Nile to Gondokoro

Wanders around Europe... In charge of constructing a railway in the Balkans... Marries Florence von Sass... Dreams of finding the source of the Nile... Sets off from Cairo... Spends a year in the Sudan... Explores the Blue Nile... Reaches Khartoum and then Gondokoro... Meets Speke and Grant returning home... Baker promises to trace the river between Lake Victoria and an unknown lake.

Without a settled home in England, Baker wandered sadly round Europe, visiting the battlefields of the Crimea and hunting wild boar in Turkey. He finally found a job to occupy his thoughts, taking charge of the construction of a railway link between the Danube and the Black Sea. This was completed by 1860, when Baker met the woman who was to become his second wife, a young, courageous and beautiful Hungarian called Florence von Sass.

By now, he had a new dream. He was a friend of John Hanning Speke, and knew that Speke and Grant were at that moment in Africa trying to discover the true source of the Nile. With typical boldness and imagination, Baker decided to set off for Lakes Victoria and Tanganyika from the north, following the Nile from Cairo, and hoping to meet his friend on the way, perhaps at the southernmost point of civilization, Gondokoro. Big game hunting, you can be sure, was not far from his mind as well.

Portraits of Sam and Florence. Florence accompanied Sam on his expedition to find the source of the Nile.

The Bakers riding camels on their journey across a desert.

Florence was determined to accompany him. A white woman in central Africa was almost unheard of in those days, but she proved to be an ideal companion, being brave, tough and resourceful. Her beauty and her persuasive words often got them out of a tight spot.

The Bakers explore the Sudan

They set off from Cairo early in 1861. Like all Baker's expeditions, this one was expensively equipped, with plenty of guns, instruments and camping gear, and the best tinned foods from Fortnum and Mason. Baker also made sure he had supplies to spare for Speke and Grant.

He decided to spend the first year getting to know the Sudan and learning the language, Arabic. After an exhausting journey by boat and on foot, they reached Berber, and explored the valleys of the Nile's chief tributary, the Blue Nile.

It was not long before Baker began to enjoy hunting game that was new to him. He shot a hippo and liked its meat: a meal made from a wild ass was less successful, and gave the party violent indigestion. He was also thrilled to watch the local tribesmen hunting. One old man was famous for catching hippo with a harpoon. Another tribe hunted elephants and

Khartoum and the Nile. It was from here that the Bakers started their journey down the river to Gondokoro.

Arab tribesmen using long swords to attack an elephant.

rhinos, armed with only huge swords.

When he felt sufficiently prepared, Baker marched on to Khartoum. There he hired boats and porters and carried on upriver. But the journey was a slow and tedious one, for they had to hack their way through the tangled swamp known as the Sudd. This mass of weeds and ferns was thick in enough places for elephants to walk on, and was an ideal breeding ground for snakes and insects.

The Bakers were glad to reach Gondokoro, even though it was a squalid and noisy place. They had only been there a fortnight, however, when the crackle of celebratory gunfire in the distance heralded the arrival of Speke and his party. Baker welcomed them and gave them supplies. He listened in fascination to Speke's account of the discovery of the Ripon Falls, though secretly he was disappointed that he himself had not been the first to the source of the Nile.

One thing puzzled Speke. Did the river which poured out of Lake Victoria over the Ripon Falls flow into another great lake before entering the Nile proper? He had heard stories of a lake to the west, but had not had time to explore it. Giving Baker as much information as he could, Speke begged him to check, so that he would be able to confirm his own theories back in London.

Lake Albert: source of the Nile?

In 1863, the Bakers and their small band of servants and grumpy porters set off. For their own safety, they had to travel under the protection of a party of Arab slave traders, and this meant that progress was slow. At first, the Arabs despised their white companions, but Sam quickly won their respect with his hunting skills and his medicine chest, and Florence impressed them with her beauty and kindness.

At last they reached the kingdom ruled by Kamrasi, whom Speke had met almost a year earlier. This wily king was more concerned with wheedling presents out of his visitors than with helping them find the lake. When he finally let them go, he asked an astonished Baker to leave his wife behind. The fearless explorer immediately clapped his revolver to Kamrasi's head, and the king backed down.

Lake Albert's discovery

The final stage of the journey to the lake was the most gruelling for the travellers, already suffering from malaria. Florence collapsed with sunstroke and had to be carried, half-dead, on a litter. But after another month they were rewarded by the sight of the huge lake glittering below them.

Sam meeting native chiefs on entering the kingdom ruled by Kamrasi.

The Bakers travel with Arabs to Kamrasi's kingdom ... The King wants Baker to leave his wife behind ... Gruelling journey to the lake ... Baker names it Lake Albert ... Canoes up the lake ... Reaches the Murchison Falls ... Begins nightmare journey home ... Stranded in Bunyoro ... Rescued by Arab traders ... The return to Gondokoro ... Across the Sudd to Suez.

An escort furnished by Kamrasi to accompany the Bakers on their journey to Lake Albert.

Baker had achieved his objective, and found what he thought was the source of the Nile. He named it Lake Albert, after Queen Victoria's husband, who had recently died. Now, low in supplies and weak with fever, he would have liked to have set off for Cairo again. But Baker was a deeply honourable man, and he intended first to fulfil his promise to Speke, and look for a river which might link the vast Lake Victoria with his own discovery.

He managed to hire some dugout canoes and oarsmen to row the party to the northern end of the lake. However, on the first night, the rowers ran away. As always, Baker was undaunted, and urged his men to

Sam's canoe, no more than a hollowed-out tree trunk, in the middle of a fearful storm on Lake Albert.

The Murchison Falls, about 37 metres (120 feet) high, from the Victoria Nile to the level of Lake Albert.

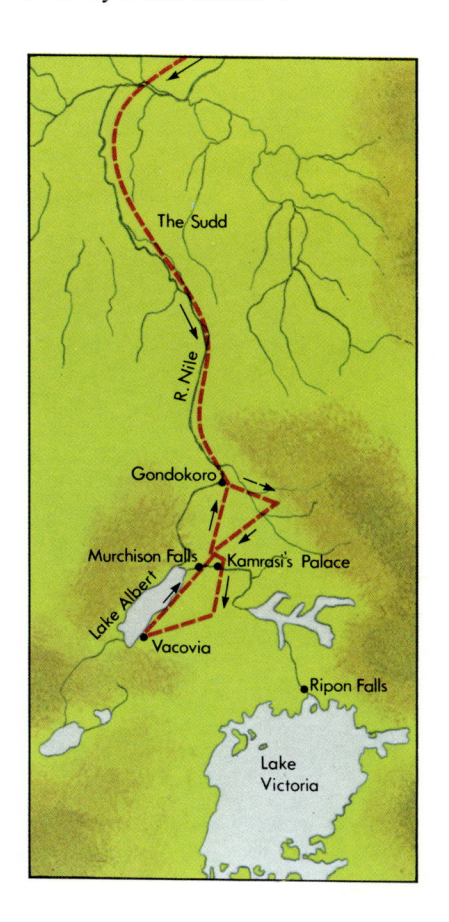

take up the oars themselves. He made makeshift rudders and even, at one point, used his huge plaid cloak as a sail. His indomitable courage took the party safely to the head of the lake through attacks by storms, crocodiles and malaria. It was plain to see where the Nile entered from Lake Victoria, and Baker followed the river as far as a fierce cataract which he named the Murchison Falls.

The return journey

At last their quest was over. But getting home proved an even greater nightmare than the journey out. With little food, few porters or guides, and hardly any trading goods, they had to ask Kamrasi for help. But he was busy fighting a war, and the Bakers were stuck in a filthy hut for months, weak from fever and hunger.

They were saved, yet again, by the appearance of the same Arab trader whom they had journeyed out with. They obtained food and porters from him, and followed his vast caravan (of over 700 men) on the slow trek north. The ever-resourceful Baker even managed to cure his crippling malaria by distilling a kind of whisky from sweet potatoes.

They entered Gondokoro in 1865, two years after they had left there. But to their sorrow there was no one to welcome them—they had been given up as dead. So Baker had to set about hiring more boats, and the party hacked its way through the horrors of the Sudd once again. When at last they reached Suez, Baker's first act was to order a tankard of iced English beer—something he had been dreaming of for a long time!

Map showing the course of the Nile and the route the Bakers took on their journey to Lake Albert.

27

Baker conquers the Nile basin

Triumphant return to England... Becomes a national hero... Invited to lead a new expedition to annex the Nile basin... After delays, finally reaches Gondokoro... Establishes a stronghold... A thousand Egyptians desert... Marches south to Masindi... Sets up a camp... Attacked by King Kabarega... Baker is forced to retreat... The area is finally secured... Retirement.

The Bakers found an ecstatic reception waiting for them in England. In 1865, Baker was awarded the Gold Medal of the Royal Geographical Society, and was knighted a year later. Despite his own excitement at finding Lake Albert, however, the question of the Nile's source was not yet settled. Richard Burton, for one, continued his bitter attack on the theories of Speke (now dead) and Baker, even suggesting that neither Lake Victoria nor Lake Albert existed!

But Sir Samuel Baker was a national hero, known to everyone as 'Baker of the Nile', and his accounts of his travels were runaway bestsellers. He settled down with his family in Norfolk, but life soon became too dull for this man of action, and he was delighted when he was asked to lead a new expedition down the Nile to annex the Nile basin area around Gondokoro on behalf of the Egyptian Government.

Baker saw the coming of civilization to this wild region as the best way to get rid of the many slave traders, and to bring peace among the warring tribes.

The 'Forty Thieves', a band of sharpshooters that Sam picked out to be his bodyguard.

The official annexation of Gondokoro on behalf of the Egyptian Government.

In fact, the Egyptian Government was not very helpful, for when he arrived in Khartoum once again in 1869, he found that most of the promised stores and boats were not there. Worse still, he found the soldiers were a rabble of convicts and escaped slaves. He did his best to smarten them up, and picked out a small band of sharpshooters to be his bodyguard, which became known as the 'Forty Thieves'.

King Kabarega attacks

Eventually, the force moved off upriver. The countryside around had been laid waste by the slavers, who were transporting more than 50,000 slaves along the Nile every year. Just as depressing was the Sudd, which was now even thicker than before. After two months of hacking, Baker was forced to turn back and wait for the river to rise. At the second attempt, they got through, with the loss of many men and boats, and marched with full colours into Gondokoro.

Here he established his stronghold, and set out to subdue the surrounding countryside. The camp was frequently attacked, and Baker retaliated by raiding nearby villages. In this way, he built up a

The Battle of Masindi where Kabarega's forces were defeated by Sam's troops.

valuable stock of grain and cattle. It was soon to be desperately needed.

The first major disaster struck when more than a thousand of the Egyptian troops deserted, taking most of the sailing boats. Now Baker had only 500 men left to face the hostile thousands all around him. His best chance of making the area peaceful was to set up a chain of forts. So, in 1872, he set out with half his men and marched south. Despite trouble with mutineers, he pushed on into Bunyoro, now ruled by Kabarega, and marched boldly into the capital Masindi.

Kabarega saw Baker as a direct threat to his kingdom, and was alarmed by the speed with which the invaders set up camp. Before long, they had erected government buildings and planted cotton bushes. Kabarega was determined to get rid of Baker, but was scared of the discipline and sharp bayonets of his soldiers. So he sent them a gift of poisoned cider, which caused widespread sickness among the men. The king's warriors attacked at dawn, but Baker swiftly brought his rifles to bear on

The 'Forty Thieves' advancing at full speed with fixed bayonets against the slave traders in Fatiko.

Sam and Florence in retirement on a visit to the Mediterranean island of Cyprus.

them, and sent rockets to burn down the king's village. His quick wits had saved him yet again, and Kabarega ran away, but it was clear that Baker would have to retreat while he could.

Throughout the terrifying march back, Baker's small force was harried, and they could hear war drums beating all around them. As they were reaching Fatiko, they were fired on by some slave traders, but a thrilling bayonet charge by the 'Forty Thieves' soon cleared the town. Here, Baker finally established himself, recruiting more troops, building a fort, and eventually defeating Kabarega.

Baker and his wife returned to England in 1873, having completed the job they had set out to do. Although slavery was still carried on around the Nile basin, its scale was greatly reduced, and trade with the outside world had been encouraged. Baker lived to a ripe old age, and even in retirement, he could not resist spending every winter abroad—shooting tigers in India, deer in Japan and bears in the Rocky Mountains of North America. He died peacefully in his country house in Devon in 1893.

Dates and events

1821 Samuel White Baker born in Gloucestershire.
1843 Marries his childhood sweetheart.
1845 The Bakers leave Mauritius for Ceylon, and establish a settlement at Nuwara Eliya.
1853 Sam returns to England. Soon after his wife dies of typhoid.
1860 Meets Florence von Sass while constructing a railway in the Balkans.
1861 Sets off from Cairo to meet Speke at Gondokoro.
1863 Leaves Gondokoro for Lake Albert.
1864 Discovers and names Lake Albert (14th March).
1865 Sam is awarded the Royal Geographical Society's Gold Medal.
1866 Knighted in England.
1869 Arrives in Khartoum to annex the Nile basin for the Egyptian Government.
1872 Battle of Masindi, Bunyoro (8th June).
1873 Returns to England and retirement.
1893 Dies peacefully near Newton Abbot in Devon.

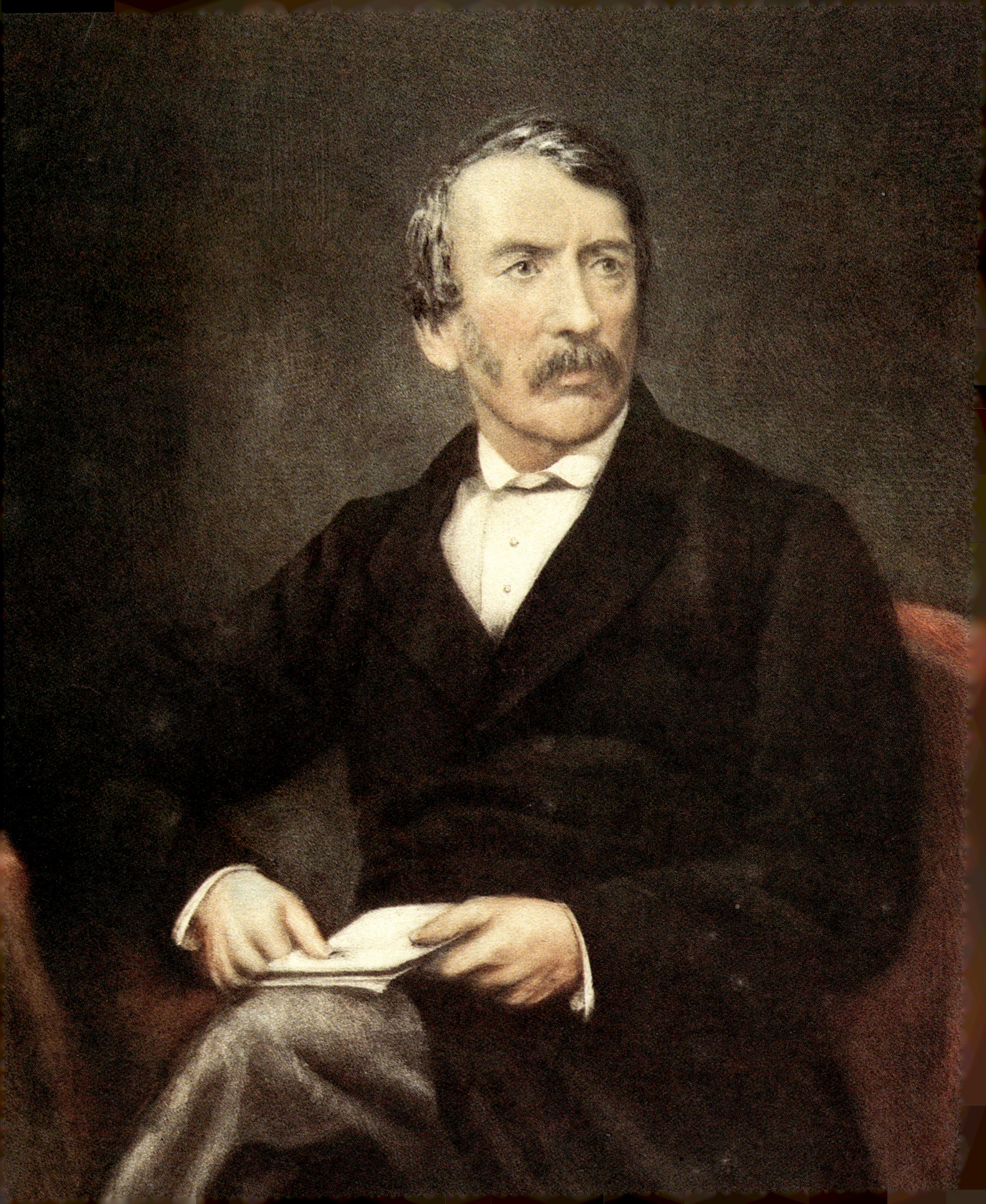

David Livingstone

Livingstone went to Africa as a missionary. Discouraged by the difficulty of converting Africans, he turned, instead, to exploring: by opening up Africa to traders, he believed the slave trade could be stamped out. In England, news of his journeys made him an almost legendary figure, yet he made few discoveries and never found the source of the Nile. Despite this he has become one of the most famous explorers in history.

Few great men have had such a hard beginning as David Livingstone. He was born in 1813 near Glasgow, and his parents were so poor that the whole family of seven had to live in one small room. David was sent out to work in the nearby cotton mill when he was only ten years old. It was backbreaking and exhausting work, which lasted from six in the morning until eight o'clock at night; only Sunday was free. The mill was very hot, and the job of the little boys—to make sure that the cotton threads did not break—entailed hours of stooping and crawling around dangerous machinery. Any mistakes were punished with a beating.

Even at this age, and in such appalling conditions, David proved that he was exceptionally determined. It is astonishing that anyone should want to go to school after such a day's work; but he did, and then read until midnight when he got home. In this way, he learned to read and write, and even began to learn Latin.

By the age of twenty-one, Livingstone had virtually educated himself, spurred on by the deep religious faith instilled in him by his father. The crucial moment of his life came when he read a pamphlet calling for missionary doctors to work in China: he decided that this was to be his vocation.

Before he could become a missionary, Livingstone had to train as a doctor at Glasgow University. He was then instructed in missionary work by the London Missionary Society. By 1840, his preparations were complete. He could not go to China because of the Opium Wars which had broken out between China and Britain the year before but, inspired by a meeting with the famous missionary Robert Moffat, he saw Africa as his goal. So, with his head full of ideals, he left his slum home for ever and sailed to Cape Town.

A portrait of Robert Moffat, the man who inspired Livingstone to do missionary work in Africa.

The first Englishman to cross Africa

When he finally reached Kuruman, 600 miles (960 km) to the north of Cape Town, he was shocked. Even though Moffat had been stationed there for twenty years, none of the local tribesmen seemed to have been converted to Christianity, and the town was nothing more than a small dirty village.

In the next three years, Livingstone made several trips to the north, trying to convert more isolated tribes, but with no success. However, this experience helped him to understand the African character better than anyone before him, and led him eventually to give up his original ideas of being a missionary. By exploring, and by opening up the heart of 'darkest Africa' to traders, he now believed that he could stamp out the slave trade and encourage white settlers.

His ambitions were delayed when he was attacked by a lion and badly mauled. He made a quick recovery, but his left arm was always weak afterwards. At this time he also became engaged to Moffat's daughter Mary. It was not a love match, but she was used to missionary life, and would be company for the lonely Livingstone.

As his missionary work seemed more hopeless, Livingstone became restless. When he heard of a large lake to the north, he quickly began to organize

Arrives in Africa... Fails to convert local tribes to Christianity ... Wants to open up central Africa... Attacked by a lion ... Marries Mary Moffat... Discovers Lake Ngami... Sends family back to England... Explores the Zambesi river... Discovers the Victoria Falls... Crosses Africa... Returns to England ... Wined and dined by London society... No time for his family.

Livingstone's escape from an attack by a lion. Although he survived the mauling, his left arm was left permanently weak.

an expedition. In 1849 he made his first trip across the arid Kalahari desert, and found the lake, which the natives called Ngami.

This was a relatively small discovery, but Livingstone became convinced that there was a large river farther north. He saw this river as the ideal way of bringing European trade to central Africa, and became obsessed with finding it.

By now he had little consideration for his family, and thought only of Africa. After sending them back to England (where they had neither home nor money, but were at least safe from malaria), he reached the river he had been seeking, the Zambesi, and made a new base at Linyanti. Greatly excited, he set about

Livingstone's arrival at Lake Ngami. Its discovery spurred him on to make further explorations.

The spectacular Victoria Falls. It was discovered by Livingstone on his journey down the Zambesi.

exploring the river. With a small party of tribesmen, he battled westwards against the jungle, hostile natives, and attacks of malaria and dysentery, and reached the Atlantic coast six months later.

England's hero

Livingstone realized immediately that this route to central Africa was too dangerous for traders. So, after recovering from his crippling illnesses, he returned to Linyanti, and set off downstream towards the east coast. On the way, he discovered a huge and dramatic waterfall, which he called the Victoria Falls. This, as far as he could see, was the only major obstacle to boats travelling up the river. By 1856, he had crossed the entire continent, becoming the first Englishman to do so.

Livingstone encountered many dangers during his explorations. Here a hippo is threatening to overturn his canoe.

At the coast, Livingstone found a Royal Navy ship which had been sent to take him back to England, where he had become an almost legendary figure. Much of what was written about him was misleading —he was thought to have converted many Africans to Christianity, for example, and many regarded him as a saintly hero.

In London, he was wined and dined and showered with medals and other awards. He could hardly walk down the street without his weather-beaten face and famous cap being recognized. It is sad that he could find little time to visit his unhappy wife and children.

The Zambesi expedition fails

It was not long before Livingstone returned to Africa. The British Government was very interested in his ideas for opening up a trading route along the Zambesi, and of starting a white colony in the fertile highlands to the north. They appointed Livingstone as a roving British Consul, and made him leader of an expedition to take a steamer up the river to search for suitable settlement sites.

Livingstone set out in 1858, accompanied by his wife and seven other Europeans. But the journey was a disaster from the beginning. The small steamer was slow, cramped and used a vast amount of fuel. The crew were struck down by malaria and dysentery. Livingstone himself turned out to be a very poor leader, refusing to admit any mistakes, having no

A portrait of Livingstone. His exploits in Africa made him an almost legendary figure.

Livingstone leads expedition up Zambesi . . . Difficulties from the start . . . Rapids force a change of plan . . . Explores Shire river . . . Reaches Lake Nyasa . . . Missionaries killed by malaria . . . Wife dies . . . Forced to give up expedition . . . Returns to England . . . Attends Burton's meeting in Bath . . . Invited to lead another expedition to Nile's source . . . Believes source is south of Lake Albert.

A photograph of Bishop Mackenzie taken before he left England to do missionary work in Africa.

sympathy for his sick men, and, in the end, hardly speaking to anyone.

Worse still, he had not prepared for the difficulties that were to face them. He had not thought of the danger of malaria, and was horrified to find that the river was blocked by rapids only a few hundred miles from the coast. No trading ships would be able to get past them. Frantically, Livingstone changed his plans, and set off up a major tributary of the Zambesi, called the Shire, only to find that this too was blocked by rapids. It seemed as though all of his dreams were to be shattered.

Whilst exploring the Shire, Livingstone made the one solid achievement of the trip: reaching the mighty Lake Nyasa. But he was not the first white man there, for the Portuguese had already established it as a centre for slave-trading. As a last-ditch effort, Livingstone ordered a steamboat to be sent from England in sections, so that it could be carried beyond the rapids and assembled by the lake.

Livingstone at work on his journal—a detailed record of his explorations in Africa.

Meanwhile, tragedy struck all around him. Bishop Mackenzie arrived from England, encouraged by Livingstone's enthusiasm for the region, and set up a missonary station. But he and his followers soon died of malaria. Mary Livingstone, after a long and miserable marriage, also died of the fever. Progress up the river became nearly impossible, and there was a constant threat of mutiny. Already two of the Europeans had resigned and Livingstone had sacked two more in a fit of rage.

Finally they were forced to give up and return to England, leaving the expedition a complete failure. This time there was no hero's welcome. To add to the sorrow of his wife's death, Livingstone now learnt that his eldest son Robert had died of wounds in the American Civil War.

Starving slaves abandoned by their Arab masters because they couldn't march any further.

Livingstone's mistake

Soon, however, a new project had claimed all his energies and attention. He was present at the meeting in Bath in 1864, at which Speke and Burton were to have their debate about the source of the Nile. Speke's unfortunate death made the whole Nile question even more sensational, and Sir Roderick Murchison invited Livingstone to return to Africa for a final attempt at settling the matter.

Livingstone began to work out his own theories. He could not believe Speke's claim that the Nile flowed out of Lake Victoria. After all, hadn't Sir Samuel Baker just returned after proving that it flowed out of Lake Albert? Livingstone, like many others at the time, rejected the idea that the two lakes were connected. He was sure that he would find the true source somewhere south of Lake Albert, perhaps in Lake Tanganyika. It was a mistake that would lead to his death in 1873.

The fatal quest for the source of the Nile

From Zanzibar to Lake Nyasa... Livingstone ill with dysentery... Reaches Lake Tanganyika... Accepts help from Arab slave-traders... Convinced that River Lualaba is the Nile's source... Forced to detour to Ujiji... Shocked by slave massacre... Meets Stanley... Proves that Lake Tanganyika is not Nile's source... Dies on bid to trace River Luabala.

Like Speke and Burton before him, Livingstone began his journey near Zanzibar, but he landed on the coast many miles farther south. His party was very small, with less than forty porters, some of them Indians recruited in Bombay. There were no Europeans, for Livingstone hated travelling with other white men: his closest companion was a little poodle called Chitane.

As usual, the going was slow. They had to hack their way through thick jungle, and many of the Indians were more interested in stealing than in marching. When they reached Lake Nyasa, there were only twelve porters left, and Livingstone was once again suffering from dysentery. He was to be almost permanently ill for the rest of his wandering life.

The situation was made even worse by the theft of his medicine box—without quinine, he had nothing to cure him of the malaria that was bound to strike. His food was running low and, to cap it all, his much-loved poodle drowned while they were crossing a river. But Livingstone's superhuman determination

Livingstone's porters are thrown into disarray by a herd of wild buffaloes.

Chitapanga, a tribal chief, receiving Livingstone with great respect and ceremony.

Livingstone, weak with fever, travelling with a native escort.

kept the expedition going and, a year after leaving the coast, he stumbled into a village on the southern shore of Lake Tanganyika.

Here, despite his views on slavery, he was glad to accept help from some Arab traders. Without their food and medicine, he might well have died of fever. While resting, he was excited to hear of another, smaller lake to the west. When at last he was able to travel there, he found to his delight, that there was a broad river flowing out of the northern end. This river, called the Lualaba, seemed the obvious answer to the age-old question. As it flowed north, where else could it go but to Lake Albert, and there become the Nile?

Slave massacre

It was an easy mistake to make. Livingstone could not possibly have known that the Lualaba never went near Lake Albert, but veered sharply westwards, ending up as the River Congo. But by now all the explorer's failing strength was devoted to proving his theory.

First of all, Livingstone had to discover the Lualaba's source. Travelling farther south, he found a larger lake: this, he was sure was the beginning of the mighty Nile. Obviously his next task was to follow the course of the Lualaba to make sure that it

A view of Ujiji, a town on the shores of Lake Tanganyika. It was here that Livingstone met Stanley in 1872.

did flow into Lake Albert. But by now he was dangerously short of food and medicines, and he was forced to make a detour to Ujiji on the shores of Lake Tanganyika, where he knew supplies would be waiting for him.

As well as fever and dysentery, Livingstone now had pneumonia in his right lung, and was coughing up blood. He had to be carried the last miles to Ujiji on a stretcher. At Ujiji, yet another disaster awaited them: their supplies, which had been sent up from the coast, had been ransacked. There were no letters, no food, no trade goods and, worst of all, no medicine.

This was a crushing blow, but Livingstone would not give in. After resting for a few months, he trekked to the village of Nyangwe, on the banks of the Lualaba. Here he was profoundly shocked when he witnessed a massacre of slaves: more than 500 natives were killed by Arab traders, or drowned in the panic. Livingstone wrote: 'It gave me the impression of being in hell.'

The famous meeting

His reports of this incident, together with the other dispatches he had been sending to the British Government, caused a horrified outcry at home. Although Britain had abolished the slave trade in her Empire as long ago as 1833, there were still many slave markets, and slave ships on the seas. After Livingstone's revelations, the British put pressure on the Sultan of Zanzibar, who closed his slave market in 1873.

The dispirited Livingstone returned to Ujiji. By this time he was without supplies, and was forced to beg from the very Arab traders whose slavery activities he loathed. It seemed that there was no way he could carry on with his quest. Then, to his astonishment, he heard that a white man was travelling to Ujiji. Three days later, amid wild celebrations, the stranger appeared and, seeing the ragged explorer, uttered the most famous words in the history of exploration: 'Doctor Livingstone, I presume?'

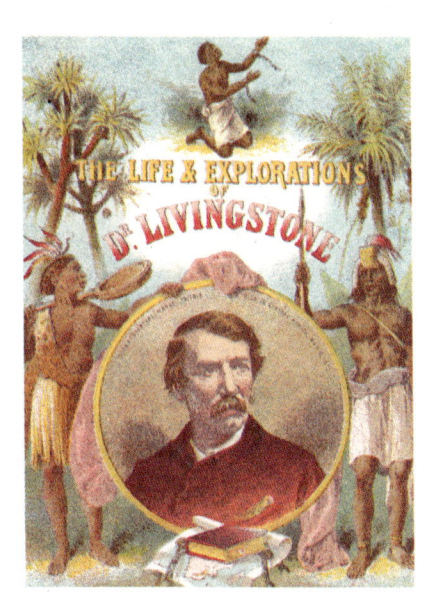

The frontispiece to The Life and Explorations of Dr Livingstone.

This church was built on the site of the old slave market in Zanzibar.

Stanley and Livingstone on Lake Tanganyika discovering that a river flows into the lake.

The stranger was Henry Morton Stanley, a journalist who had been sent out to Africa to discover if Livingstone was still alive. Stanley's great journey, and his portrait of Livingstone in the bush, were to cause a sensation back in England, and restore the doctor's heroic name. His expedition was lavishly equipped, and was able to supply Livingstone with all he needed.

The final journey

Most important of all, Stanley's arrival cheered Livingstone by showing that he had not been forgotten by the outside world. He soon grew fond of Stanley—here was one white man he did not squabble with. Together they made a short trip to the northern end of Lake Tanganyika, where they found a river

Livingstone being carried in a litter to the village of Chitambo.

Map showing the position of Chitambo, the village where Livingstone died.

flowing *into* the lake. Here at last was positive proof that Lake Tanganyika could not be a source of the Nile.

Although he was sad to see Stanley go (early in 1873), Livingstone was now more determined than ever to trace the Lualaba. After waiting for more stores and porters to arrive from the coast, he headed south once again for the lake at the source of the river.

But years of hard travel, disease and poor food had taken their toll, and soon Livingstone was weaker than ever. The eastern side of the lake was a wilderness of mud and swamps, and they scarcely covered two miles a day. Finally they reached the village of Chitambo, where he collapsed, and died two days later.

His few remaining followers embalmed his body and carried it back to the coast, where it was loaded onto a British warship. The explorer was given a hero's funeral and buried in Westminster Abbey, where his grave can still be seen.

Dates and events

- 1813 David Livingstone born in Low Blantyre, Scotland.
- 1840 Leaves for South Africa after being ordained by the London Missionary Society.
- 1849 First trip across the Kalahari desert to Lake Ngami.
- 1856 Returns to England after crossing the entire African continent.
- 1858 Appointed roving British Consul in Africa and explores the Zambesi.
- 1864 Livingstone is invited by Sir Roderick Murchison to settle the Nile question once and for all.
- 1865 Livingstone sails from Folkestone.
- 1866 Reaches Zanzibar.
- 1868 Discovers Lake Bangweolo.
- 1869 Arrives in Ujiji.
- 1871 Livingstone is horrified by a slave massacre at Nyangwe. Meets Stanley in Ujiji.
- 1872 Livingstone sets off on last journey.
- 1873 Dies in Chitambo, on the shores of Lake Bangweolo (1st May).

STANLEY IN AFRICA.

Henry Morton Stanley

> 'Doctor Livingstone, I presume?' These words by Stanley have become the most famous in exploration history. Although renowned for finding Livingstone, his finest achievement was to prove that Lake Victoria was the source of the Nile. In later years he opened up the Congo basin for the Belgians and led a nightmare mission to rescue Emin Pasha. From a brash journalist, Stanley developed into the greatest of all Africa's explorers.

Stanley's childhood and youth read like a novel by Charles Dickens. It is difficult to find out the true facts, because his own account of his early years is often highly coloured to boost his image. For a start, his real name was not Henry Stanley but John Rowlands. He was born in north Wales in 1841, the illegitimate son of a farmer. He never knew his father, and his mother soon disowned him, so from the age of six he was brought up in the local workhouse. This lack of parental love scarred him for life.

In his autobiography he claims that he ran away from the workhouse after giving a severe beating to a sadistic master; but the truth is probably that he left by agreement. After months of unhappy drifting, he reached Liverpool, where he signed on as cabin boy on a ship bound for New Orleans. Having crossed the Atlantic, he jumped ship and soon got a job as a clerk.

His luckiest break in life was to be adopted by a rich merchant—named Henry Stanley. He was educated by him, and given a home and the first period of love and security he had known. But the young man's fiery temper eventually got the better of him, and he was sent away, never to see his new father again. By 1861, he was off on his wanderings again. The American Civil War had broken out, and Stanley soon joined up with the Confederate Army.

A Confederate attack. Stanley joined the Confederates and was captured fighting his first battle.

Over the next eight years, Stanley wandered far and wide in a search to prove himself to the world. He was short, but strong and very determined to be a success: so determined that many found him arrogant. At first, he only met with failure. He was captured in his first battle for the Confederates. After being released from the misery of prisoner-of-war camp, he worked his passage back to Liverpool.

But there was no warm welcome awaiting him in England. Once again his mother turned him away,

50

James Gordon Bennett, the owner of the New York Herald.

and with this final rejection he returned to America. His own account of his subsequent adventures are exciting, but probably exaggerated. He became a clerk in the navy, and in one battle claimed to have swum, under heavy fire, to attach a rope to an enemy ship. After deserting from the navy, he went west to become a gold prospector, but failed to make his fortune. Then, he planned a trip around the world, but this was abandoned when he was beaten up and robbed in Turkey.

Stanley's mission

Back in the United States once more, he finally found a job that he excelled at—journalism. His toughness, ambition and flair with words made him an ideal war correspondent. His first commission was to report on the war against the Indian tribes in Kansas. Stanley was saddened by the savagery of the white men, and became very sympathetic towards the oppressed tribesmen.

His first sensational 'scoop' was about the British invasion of Abyssinia in 1868. After the capital Magdala had fallen, Stanley hurried back to Suez ahead of the other journalists, and bribed the telegraph officer to send his reports out before even those of the British commanding officer! By some accident, the telegraph line then went dead, leaving Stanley's paper, the *New York Herald*, as the only one with the news.

Stanley was now a famous reporter, and travelled widely in Europe. Whilst he was covering the Civil War in Spain, he even found time to take his astonished mother and sister on holiday to Paris. It was in Paris that he was summoned by the owner of the *Herald*, James Gordon Bennett. Bennett's orders were simple: 'Find Livingstone!'

Stanley finds Livingstone in Ujiji

Livingstone forgotten and presumed dead . . . Leads expedition to find him . . . Overcomes a mutiny . . . Historic meeting with Livingstone . . . Together they go to Lake Tanganyika . . . The Nile's source is not found there . . . Stanley returns to Zanzibar with Livingstone's journals . . . Mixed reception in Europe . . . Pallbearer at Livingstone's funeral . . . Decides to return to Africa to settle Nile question.

It was bold of Bennett to send his best reporter out to Africa. Livingstone had been largely forgotten by the world, and had been reported as dead. Bennett saw that he might create a sensation if Stanley was successful in his mission, so he gave him unlimited financial backing.

When he reached Zanzibar in 1871, Stanley immediately set about organizing his expedition on a lavish scale, taking with him over 200 porters and 6 tonnes of supplies, including an enamel bath and a Persian carpet. He set off as soon as possible towards Lake Tanganyika, driving his men hard. Unlike the gentle Livingstone, Stanley believed in physical force to keep his men going, and in quelling any mutinies.

Stanley and his porters wading through a swamp on their journey to find Livingstone.

But even he needed all his determination and optimism to overcome, among other things, a plot against his life by some porters, a swamp where the mud came up to his neck, and a crocodile who almost dragged him into the water. He was weak with fever and dysentery, and feared that Livingstone might be dead. Even if he found him, he had been warned by John Kirk, the British Consul in Zanzibar, that Livingstone was such a touchy man that he might not want to talk.

All his fears vanished when he entered Ujiji and shook the white-haired doctor by the hand. The two soon became fond of each other, Livingstone looking upon Stanley as a son. Together they made a short journey to Lake Tanganyika, and confirmed that it could not be the source of the Nile. After four months, Stanley had to leave, but he was unable to persuade the doctor to return with him to the coast. Ensuring that Livingstone was well supplied, Stanley made a swift march to Zanzibar, carrying with him Livingstone's precious last letters and journals.

Stanley and Livingstone greeting one another in Ujiji.

Unpopularity in England

When the news of his great expedition broke in Europe, there was an immediate controversy. Many people congratulated Stanley on his magnificent achievement, but the newspapers disliked this brash young American journalist. Some even suggested that his account of meeting Livingstone was a hoax! The Royal Geographical Society, too, were jealous that their most famous explorer had been rescued by a mere journalist.

When Livingstone's body arrived back in England, Stanley was invited to be one of the pallbearers at the funeral. The unpleasantness was beginning to blow over, and Stanley now saw his mission as trying to complete Livingstone's work and succeeding where so many others had failed. First he would return to Africa and thoroughly explore all the great lakes to establish beyond any doubt which one of them fed the Nile. Then he planned to trace the course of the River Lualaba.

The two explorers on Lake Tanganyika.

The Nile question is finally settled

Backed by the London *Daily Telegraph* and the *New York Herald* with the massive sum of £12,000 (Livingstone had barely £1,500!), Stanley landed in Zanzibar. This time he was equipped even more heavily, and took over 350 porters with him, carrying, among other things, a wooden boat which could be assembled at the lakeside. He also had three English assistants.

On the journey from the coast, the huge expedition suffered the same problems as those before them: malaria, rainstorms, hostile tribesmen and constant desertions. Worst of all, there was a famine raging all around them. One of Stanley's white assistants died of typhoid and, by the time they reached Lake Victoria, barely half of the original force remained.

Undeterred, Stanley had the boat assembled, and named it 'Lady Alice', after his fiancée in New York. With ten men, he rowed up the eastern shore of the lake to the Ripon Falls, discovered by Speke thirteen years earlier. Here he visited King Mutesa, who had grown more wily and powerful than ever before, but promised an escort of war canoes. Stanley then continued his circumnavigation of the lake, pausing only to wreak terrible vengeance on a tribe that had dared to attack him. With the help of Mutesa's warriors, he opened fire and killed at least forty tribesmen.

Arrives in Zanzibar... Reaches Lake Victoria... Explores lake by boat... Proves that lake has only one outlet... Tribal war prevents exploration of Lake Albert... Sails around Lake Tanganyika and finds no outlet... Marches to River Lualaba... Sails down Lualaba... Daily attacks by natives... Near starvation... Reaches supplies at coast... Hero's welcome in England.

Stanley's wooden boat, the 'Lady Alice', was built in sections so that it could be carried by porters.

His first objective had been achieved. The lake had only one outlet—at the Ripon Falls—which had to be the Nile. He was prevented from exploring Lake Albert by a local uprising, so he turned south to Lake Tanganyika. From Ujiji, he sailed quickly around the lake, finding no outlet that could possibly be the Nile: Speke had been right all along.

An epic journey

The second and even more dangerous part of Stanley's heroic plan was to follow the course of the River Lualaba to the sea. It could not, as Livingstone had believed, be the beginning of the Nile, so it had to be the Congo, which flowed into the Atlantic over 1,500 miles (2,400 km) away.

By this time, the expedition was down to about 140 men and women. Stanley knew that he would be helpless against attacks by cannibals and other natives, so he joined force with the notorious slave-trader Tippu

Stanley burying one of his companions who had died of typhoid.

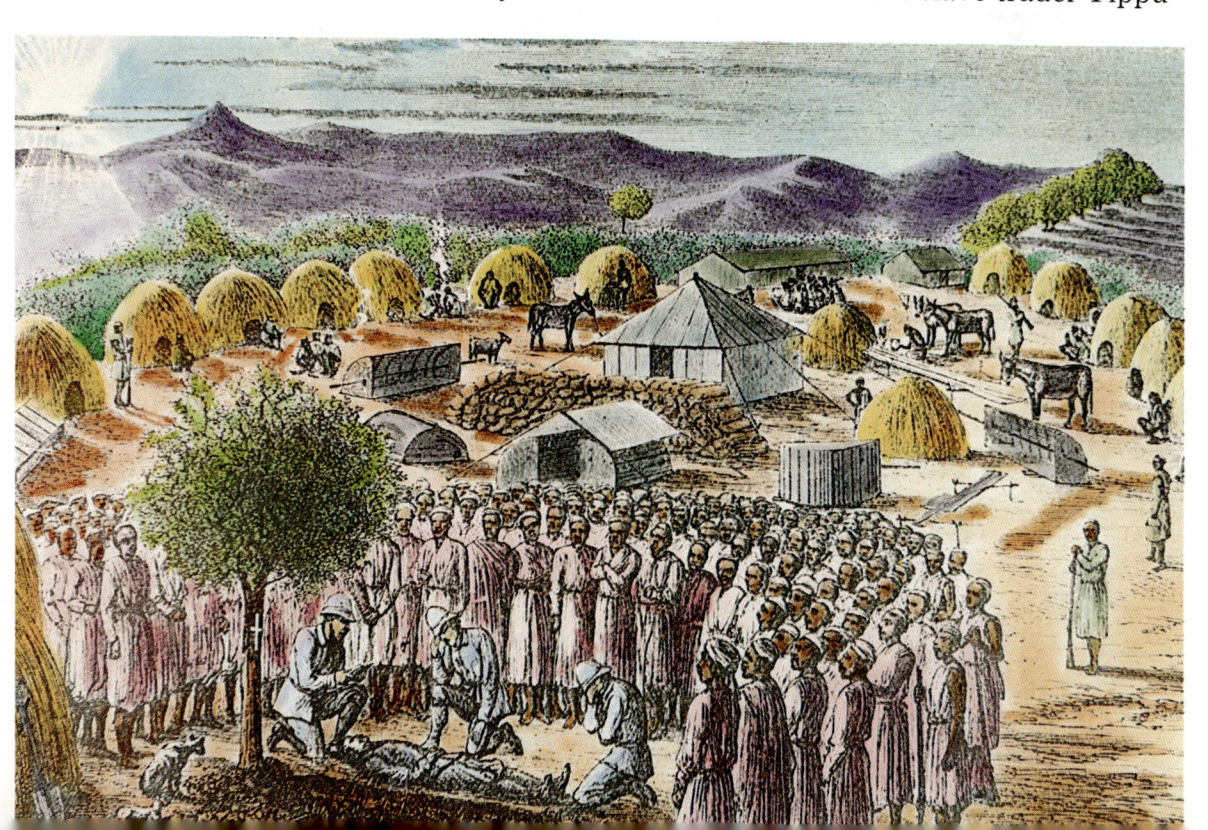

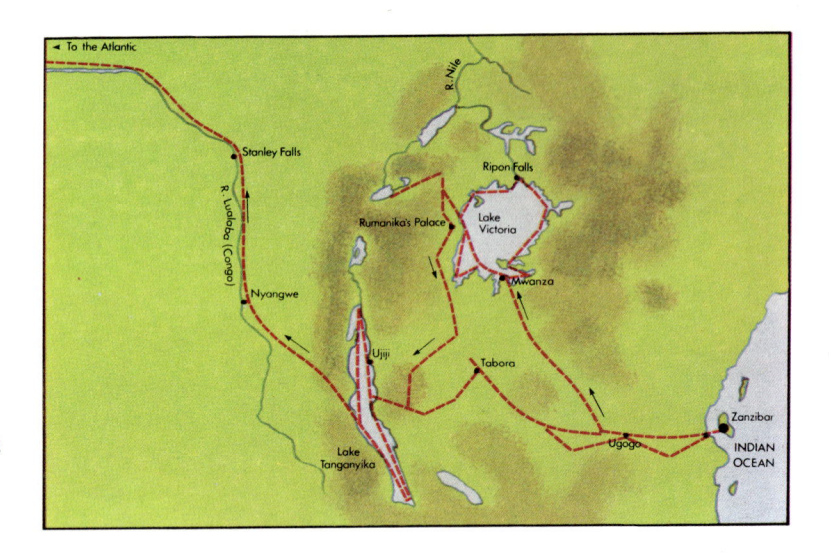

Map showing the route taken by Stanley to Lake Victoria and down the Lualaba.

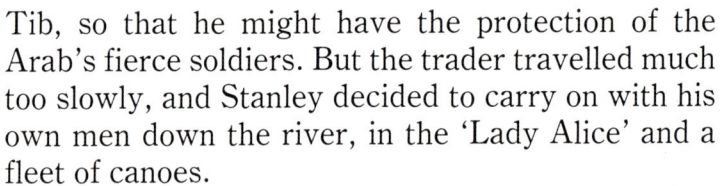

Stanley's reception by King Mutesa's body-guard on the shore of Lake Victoria.

Tib, so that he might have the protection of the Arab's fierce soldiers. But the trader travelled much too slowly, and Stanley decided to carry on with his own men down the river, in the 'Lady Alice' and a fleet of canoes.

No other European had penetrated into this savage region before, and Stanley soon found himself being constantly attacked by tribes far more bloodthirsty than he had yet encountered. At a long stretch of cataracts, they had to manhandle the boats along the bank and refloat them in calm water. The situation grew more desperate as they were attacked almost daily by hordes of up to 2,000 natives. Only the power of their rifles saved them.

Food was another problem—how could they trade with men who threw spears at them? To Stanley's relief, they at last found a peaceful and friendly tribe, and knew that they must be nearing civilization. But all too soon they came across another huge obstacle in their path—a second, and longer, stretch of waterfalls and rapids. Hauling the boats overland was by now almost impossible. By miraculous determination, they managed to cover 180 miles (290 km) —but that took five months.

Stanley's party in council in Ujiji before following the Lualaba on its course to the sea.

    Finally, half-dead, the 115 survivors crawled into a village and sent messengers ahead to the coast. Relief arrived in the nick of time, bringing food and, to Stanley's delight, three bottles of pale ale. His epic journey was over, and all that remained for him was to transport his faithful porters by ship back to Zanzibar, which they had left exactly 999 days before.

    Stanley returned to a hero's welcome in England, even from those who had previously sneered at him. The age-old question of the Nile's source had now been settled, for on top of Stanley's voyages round the lakes, General Gordon had just finished charting the entire length of the river from Cairo. The hair-raising journey down the Congo river captured the public's imagination, and Stanley's thrilling account of it in *Through the Dark Continent* was a massive bestseller.

Stanley's expedition under attack from a fleet of war canoes on the Lualaba.

Stanley's expedition to rescue Emin Pasha

Like Livingstone before him, Stanley was now obsessed with Africa. He soon became restless in London, and eventually managed to inspire King Leopold of Belgium with his ideas for colonizing the Congo. By 1879, he was back in Zanzibar, recruiting many of his faithful porters from the previous expedition. He sailed round to the Congo estuary through the Suez Canal and the Mediterranean, and set to work, in his ruthless and masterful way.

In the next three years, he supervised the building of a road from the coast, past the cataracts and up to a wide part of the upper Congo, called Stanley Pool. Five river stations were set up, and manned by Belgian officials. A steamer was carried overland from the coast and launched on the Pool. During this period, Stanley had to parley endlessly with tribal chiefs, and sign treaties with them. At one point he

Bored with city life ... Asked by Belgians to colonize the Congo ... Builds road to upper Congo ... Nearly dies from malaria ... Distressed by the arrival of slave-traders ... Returns exhausted to London ... Returns to Africa to rescue Emin Pasha in Sudan ... Pasha eventually persuaded to retreat ... Stanley returns to England in triumph ... Pasha returns to interior ... Marries ... Politics ... Death.

A band of captives being driven into slavery. Similar scenes were found by Stanley on the River Congo.

General Gordon. He was killed by the same rebels that were threatening Emin Pasha.

nearly died of malaria.

Even after all this unrelenting work, which gained Stanley the heroic nickname of 'Bula Matari', or 'Smasher of Rocks', the Belgian King begged him to stay on. But when he reluctantly returned to the Congo, he was horrified to see that the Arab slave-traders had followed in his footsteps from the east, and were ravaging the upper part of the river. It seemed as though he had opened up the Congo to the world, only to let in slavery and greed.

In 1884, he returned, exhausted, to London. He received little thanks from the Belgians, and watched the country he had hoped would turn into a great African nation being annexed by European powers. To make matters worse, his offer of marriage to an English girl was refused.

The rigours of African travel had taken their toll on Stanley. Though only in his forties, he was drawn and exhausted, and his hair was prematurely white. But, in 1886, he was called on to perform one last act of heroism. His mission was to rescue Emin Pasha, the governor of the southern Sudan, whose garrison was reported to be surrounded by rebels. It was these rebels who had stormed Khartoum and killed General Gordon four years earlier.

Stanley took this Maxim machine-gun on his mission to rescue Emin Pasha.

The meeting of Stanley and Emin Pasha. His mission to rescue Emin was the last act of heroism he was to perform in Africa.

Stanley recruited a number of British Army officers, as well as 700 other men, and armed himself with plenty of modern rifles and a machine gun. He set out from the Congo basin, and headed for Emin's camp near Lake Albert.

The expedition was an ill-fated one. Leaving half his force as a rearguard on the Congo, Stanley hurried as best he could through the dense and terrifying jungle towards Emin. When he arrived, he found to his disgust that the governor did not wish to be rescued. All Stanley's arguments were useless. In despair, he fought back through the jungle to pick up his rear column, which he found decimated by fever and desertion.

Somehow, Stanley got his pitifully depleted force back to Lake Albert. At last, Emin realized the

A portrait of Stanley in his forties. The rigours of African travel turned his hair white.

danger of his position, and agreed to accompany the relief party to Zanzibar, together with about 600 of his followers. They reached the coast at the end of 1889. On his way home, Stanley was astonished to hear that the man he had just gone so far to rescue had set off again into the interior of Africa. The whole, terrible journey seemed to have been futile.

Futile or not, it brought Stanley even more fame. In Europe, he was mobbed wherever he was seen: popular songs were written about him, and Queen Victoria invited him to dinner. Best of all, the girl who had previously refused him at last agreed to become his wife.

After his grand marriage in Westminster Abbey, Stanley was still unable to settle down. Following wildly successful lecture tours of the United States and Britain, his wife persuaded him to stand as a Member of Parliament. But he hated the stuffiness of the House of Commons, and retired as soon as he could to the Surrey countryside. He died there in 1904.

Dates and events

1841 Born John Rowlands in Denbigh, north Wales.
1859 Goes to New Orleans, where he is adopted by Henry Stanley, a wealthy merchant.
1861 Joins the Confederate Army during the American Civil War.
1868 'Scoop' story during the war in Abyssinia.
1871 Arrives in Zanzibar to find Livingstone for the *New York Herald*.
1873 Stanley leaves Livingstone after making a short journey to Lake Tanganyika.
1879 Returns to Zanzibar on the way to the Congo.
1884 Returns to London.
1886 Sets off to rescue Emin Pasha in the Sudan.
1889 Returns to England, the expedition a failure.
1890 Marries Dorothy Tennant, an actress.
1895-1900 M.P. for Lambeth.
1904 Dies in Surrey.

Glossary

Annex To take over another country, usually by force.
Bailiff Someone who manages an estate or farm in the owner's absence.
Cannibal A person or an animal who eats the flesh of his own species.
Caravan A group of people travelling together for security.
Cataract A waterfall.
Circumnavigate To sail round.
Colonize To make a country dependent on another through financial aid, etc.
Confederates The eleven southern states in the American Civil War.
Consul A person appointed by his government to look after his country's interests in a foreign land.
Delirious Extreme light-headedness associated with a fever.
Distil To extract alcohol from a liquid.
Dysentery An infection of the intestines.
Embalm To preserve a dead body from decay.
Illegitimate A person whose parents are not legally married.
Missionary A person sent abroad to convert people to his religion.
Mutiny A rebellion against a person in authority.
Pall-bearer One of the people who carries the coffin at a funeral.
Parley A conference with an enemy to establish a treaty.
Quinine A drug used to treat malaria.
'Scoop' A term in journalism when a newspaper prints a story ahead of its rivals.
Typhoid A dangerous fever.
Wanderlust An urge to travel or to move from place to place.
Wheedle To obtain something through flattery.
Workhouse A place where poor people are given shelter in return for work.

Further reading

The Blue Nile by Alan Moorehead (Harper and Row, 1974)

The White Nile by Alan Moorehead (Harper and Row, 1971)

Heroes of the Dark Continent by J. W. Buel (Arno Press, 1889)

What Led to the Discovery of the Nile by John H. Speke (Biblio Distributors, 1967)

The Man Who Presumed by Byron Farwell (Greenwood, 1974)

Stanley: An Adventurer Explored by Richard Hall (Houghton Mifflin, 1975)

Through the Wilds of Africa by A. G. Feather (Metro Books, reprint of 1890 edition)

How I Found Livingstone by H. M. Stanley (Arno Press, reprint of 1872 edition)

Livingstone by Tim Jeal (Dell, 1975)

David Livingstone: The Dark Interior by Oliver Ransford (St. Martin's Press, 1978)

Index

Baker, Florence 22, 23, 25
Baker, Sir Samuel 16, 18-31
   childhood 19
   conquers Nile basin 28-31
   death 31
   death of first wife 21
   in Ceylon 20
   in Mauritius 19
   journey to Lake Albert 25-7
   love of hunting 20-21, 22, 23, 31
   malaria 25, 27
   marches into Masindi 30
   marriage 19
   meets Grant and Speke at Gondokoro 24
   names Murchison Falls 27
Berber 23
Bruce, James 7
Buganda 14
Burton, Richard 6-7, 8-9, 10, 12, 16-17, 41, 42

Daily Telegraph 54

Fatiko 31

Gordon, General 57, 59
Gondokoro 13, 16, 22, 24, 27, 28, 29
Grant, James 12, 14, 15, 22

Kabarega, King of Bunyoro 30-31
Kamrasi, King of Bunyoro 15, 16, 27
Karagwe 14
Khartoum 16, 24, 29
Kuruman 35

Lake Albert 41, 60
Lake Nyasa 40, 42
Lake Tanganyika 10, 41, 46
Lake Victoria 10, 14, 17, 41, 54
Leopold, King of Belgium 58, 59
Livingstone, Dr David 52, 53
   character 39-40
   childhood 33
   crosses African continent 37
   death 47
   death of wife 41
   discovers Lake Ngami 36
   discovers Victoria Falls 37
   explores the Zambesi 36
   found by Stanley 45
   illness 42, 44
   marriage 35
   missionary zeal 33
   sails to Cape Town 34
   seeks source of River Lualaba 43-4, 47
   seeks source of River Nile 42-5
London Missionary Society 34

Mackenzie, Bishop 41
Malaria 25, 41, 42
Masindi 30
Moffat, Robert 34, 35
Murchison Falls 27
Murchison, Sir Robert 4, 11
Mutesa, King of Buganda 14, 15, 54

New York Herald 51, 54
Nyangwe 44

Pasha, Emin 59, 60-61
Petherick, John 13, 16

Ripon Falls 15, 17

River Congo 55-7
River Lualaba 43, 47, 53, 55
River Nile
   search for source, 7, 10, 11, 13, 24, 26, 41, 42-5, 53
   Blue Nile 7, 23
   White Nile 7
Rowlands, John
   see **Stanley, Henry Morton**
Royal Geographical Society 8, 11, 53
Rumanika, King of Karagwe 14

Slave trade 28, 29, 31, 35, 43, 45, 55-6
Speke, John Hanning 5-17, 22, 24, 28, 42, 55
   awarded Royal Geographical Society Gold Medal 16
   books published 16
   commissioned for the Punjab 5
   death 17
   discovers Lake Victoria 10
   expedition to Somalia with Burton 5, 8-9
   finds outlet from Lake Victoria 15
   names Ripon Falls 15
   public debate with Burton 17, 41
   relationship with Burton 6, 11, 12, 16-17
   schooling 5
   second expedition with Burton 9
   second trip to Lake Victoria 11, 12-15
Stanley, Henry Morton 17, 46, 49-61
   attempts to colonize Congo 58-9

Index

Stanley, H. M. *(cont.)*
 childhood 49
 death 61
 deserts from navy 51
 expedition to rescue Emin
  Pasha 58-61
 follows course of River
  Lualaba 55-7
 joins Confederate Army 49
 journey to find Livingstone
  52-3
 journey down River Congo
  56-7
 journey to find River Nile
  54-5
 marriage 61
 Member of Parliament 61
 Through the Dark Continent
  57
Sudd 24, 27, 29

Tippu Tib 56

Ujiji 44, 45, 53, 55

Victoria Falls 37

Picture acknowledgements

The publisher would like to thank all those who provided illustrations on the following pages: Mary Evans Picture Library 9, 11 (bottom), 18, 32, 34, 36, 43 (bottom), 46 (bottom), 48, 50; Alan Hutchison Library 11 (top), 24 (top), 37; Peter Jarvis *front cover* 8, 10, 13 (bottom), 14, 16, 17, 21, 23, 24 (bottom), 25, 26 (top and bottom), 27 (top), 29, 30 (top and bottom), 35, 40 (bottom), 43 (top), 44, 46 (top), 52, 53 (top and bottom), 55, 56 (bottom), 57 (top and bottom), 59 (bottom); The Mansell Collection 20, 38, 39, 40 (top), 41, 42, 45 (top), 58, 60; Richmond upon Thames Borough Council 6; Royal Geographical Society 4; Malcolm S. Walker 12, 27 (bottom), 47, 56.

SEP 1 5 1986

J920

9 IDA WILLIAMS

Langley, Andrew.
 Explorers on the Nile / Andrew Langley. -- Morristown, N.J. : Silver Burdett, [1982], c1981.
 64 p. : ill. (some col.) ; 23 cm. -- (In profile) (A Silver Burdett international library selection)
 Includes bibliographical references and index.
 Contents: John Hanning Speke -- Sir Samuel Baker -- David Livingstone -- Henry Morton Stanley.
 ISBN 0-382-06637-5

IW

R00184 35081

GA   09 JUL 86   9218066   GAPApc SEE NEXT CRD

Henry's Just a Witticism

excerpted from

Henry's Hilarious Oneliners

By Henry W. Haverstock

We Need To Laugh More so we don't surrender to the harsh realities seen in a dynamically changing world. The strain of daily living in the 1990s needs to be met with a Positive Attitude and an ability to laugh at life's absurd moments. In fact, laughter promotes good health and builds emotional bridges. Like music, laughter is a Universal Language.   *continued on page 64*

Henry's Just a Witticism
by Henry W. Haverstock

Copyright © 1992 Henry W. Haverstock

All rights reserved. No part of this book may be reproduced in whole or in part, without written permission from the publisher, except a reviewer who may quote brief passages in a review showing the logo of the cover on any page showing the quoted oneliners; nor may any part of this book be reproduced, stored in a retrieval system, or transmitted in any form or by any means electronic, mechanical, photocopying, recording, or other, without specific written permission from the publisher.

Many jokes excerpted from *Henry's Hilarious Oneliners* © 1990 by Henry W. Haverstock. Additional new jokes © herein.

Cover Art and Illustrations by Barry Lawrence
© 1991 Henry W. Haverstock
Text Design & Book Development by
Robert Parker & Associates
and Laser Set of Minnetonka

HENRY'S HILARIOUS ONELINERS is a trademark of Henry's Publishing Company Inc.

First Printing, May, 1992
ISBN 1-879916-07-X
Library of Congress Catalog Card Number 91-90330

continued from page 1

Henry's Just a Witticism gives you a laugh book, like a favorite list of songs and notes, to cheer and jeer, relaxing yourself, family, friends, and business associates—enabling everyone to get a better perspective on life.

The Quality of Life can be greatly enhanced by the use of jokes and one-liners, fun to most everyone present at a gathering of two or more, and bringing a chuckle or laugh to the individual reader. Often we forget the punch lines of jokes we have heard, or wish we had a way to make a friend laugh.

Henry's Just a Witticism offers more than 100 jokes gathered over many years by Henry W. Haverstock. This book also describes methods of gathering your own one-liners and provides space to record new jokes you have collected. You will also enjoy other books in the series: *Henry's Just a Chuckle* and *Henry's Just a Laugh*.

If you've enjoyed this sampling of Henry's collection of personal and borrowed humor, you'll really like his original book of over 800 one-liners, *Henry's Hilarious Oneliners,* printed in soft cover and hard cover editions for your permanent library. And if you'd like to give someone special a mini-book version of Henry's whimsical assortment of comedy, there are currently three titles available: *Henry's Just a Witticism, Henry's Just a Chuckle,* and *Henry's Just a Laugh.* Tuck these mini-books into your pocket, purse or briefcase for a handy reference the next time you need a little punch for your conversation, speech or meeting. Ask for them at your local bookstore.

Henry's Publishing Company, Inc.
Post Office Box 5175
Minneapolis, Minnesota 55343

A Robert Parker & Associates Book

Henry's Hilarious One-Liners

One-Liner Jokes for All Occasions

Add COLOR and ZEST To All Your Personal and Business Communications

Speeches Talks Political Conventions
Letters Family Evenings Radio and Television At the Beach Schools
Alone at Night Conversations On Desert Islands You Name It!
In Planes, Trains and...

by Henry W. Haverstock

people. Laughter promotes health; it stimulates the health—inducing endorphins. Laughter enriches every relationship: business, social, political, recreations. More laughter might also mean less crime.

To get things going, I am enclosing a complementary copy of my new book, HENRY'S HILARIOUS ONELINERS. When you have stopped laughing at the one-liner jokes (One of your own appearing at entry 792), I am sure you will see the wisdom in allowing the whole nation—and maybe the whole world—in on the importance of laughter.

I suggest the week following the April 15 income tax deadline as an appropriate one to set aside for a whole week of tension-easing laughter, while we move back into life's everyday preoccupations.

Respectfully—and hilariously—yours,

Hugh Haverstock

Henry W. Haverstock

LAW OFFICES OF
HENRY W. HAVERSTOCK

September 5, 1991

Hon. George Bush, President
United States of America
White House
Washington, D.C.

Dear President Bush:

    With so many grim events in the news on a daily basis, I submit that there is a need for a National LAUGHTER WEEK.

    Such a week might furnish a respite during which we could each take stock, and return to a more rational perspective—one which is slanted toward all the good in the world.

    Laughter is good for people. It enables us to build a more proportioned view of our lives, and that of our fellow man. Laughter, like music, is a universal language. Laughter, appropriately used, builds bridges between

heard on radio or television originally should list the show, date, station, and people identified and involved. Do not send any one-liners or jokes heard on humor shows or specials.

Include this statement, signed and dated:

"I hereby give permission for my enclosed original one-liner and/or joke to be used by Henry's Publishing Company, Minneapolis, MN 55343, in any form, and release all rights to said company without payment."

Your signature and date here.

Mail To: New One-liners
            Henry's Publishing Company, Inc.
            Post Office Box 5175
            Minneapolis, MN 55343

If we include your one-liner, we will try to credit each author with a listing. No Guarantee, but wouldn't it be fun to be published in a book?!?

You Might Become Published!

One-liners and humorous short tales that can make people laugh and be happy in this difficult and stress-filled world are heard locally in towns and cities everywhere, but often the best one-liners soon are lost to the rest of the world. You can help change that and get credit, too, for original one-liners.

Henry's Publishing Company is interested in exposing more people, especially office workers and business people, to the joys of a little chuckle or a hearty laugh to offset the serious side of daily business.

Send your ORIGINAL one-liners and jokes, heard or experienced by you, your family and friends to us at the address below, typed or printed very clearly. If we think it is funny, too, we will consider including it in a future one-liner book crediting your name, city, and state. No One-liners Will Be Returned and They Become The Property of Henry's Publishing Company, Inc. to be used solely at its discretion. Include your full name, address, and age (Those eighteen or younger, please ask one of your parents to sign a copy of the statement below).

Please, do not use one-liners from newspapers, magazines, or other printed matter. Those one-liners

My Own One-Liners

You Can Tell Your Own One-Liners

When you focus attention on the daily world around you at home, office, and even in shopping centers and at school, you can often see humorous situations and hear funny one-liners from the actual conversations. The problem is trying to remember them even when you repeat them several times to friends and family.

The answer is to write the words down carefully so you can actually repeat them months later. One-liners seem to change as you tell them to others: a word here, a phrase there, and you have a different statement...sometimes no longer funny. Try to keep the situation first seen and heard described simply in the words written. Jokes and humor often happen spontaneously. Don't trust yourself to remember without recording the words.

Use the space on the next page of this mini-book to start your collection. Better yet, look for *Henry's Hilarious Oneliners* in your bookstore. It has over 800 jokes plus pages that serve as your own personal humor scrapbook.

professionally rather than by individuals for friends. At one time, many letters had one or more cartoons drawn in the margins by pen and colored inks.

QUIP(S) – *A clever or witty remark, usually sarcastic. A quipster is the person who quips against others using verbal remarks.*

CHUCKLING – *Softly laughing to oneself; Being amused.*

BELLY LAUGH – *A loud hearty laugh usually in an informal situation, but not always; and not required to have fun.*

ONE-LINER – *A brief, witty, or humorous remark, often written on more than one line, but spoken as if just in one continous form.*

HENRY'S ONELINERS – © *copyrighted one-liners and jokes used in* Henry's Hilarious Oneliners *book and* Henry's Hilarious Postcards, Henry's Just a Laugh, Henry's Just a Chuckle, Henry's Just a Witticism.

Clips, Cartoons, and Quips

The art of the joke as an important part of social interaction has slowly disappeared. Jokes are used mostly for entertainment on radio, television, and in professional publications; and often these are contrived and usually not as funny as those spontaneous situations and spoofs we do to each other in fun. Probably the decline in personal letter writing replaced by telephone talking is why jokes and one-liners are not recorded as often in written form, and people seem to be just more serious in their daily activities. Below I have listed the dictionary meanings for those parts of jokes and one-liners that can be developed from everyday experiences.

CLIPSHEETS (CLIPS) – *Sheets of newspaper stories, articles, and jokes to be saved. Usually placed on only one side of the paper.* Clip and save!

CARTOON(S) – *A drawing caricaturing some action or subject. A sequence of drawings relating to a comic incident or a story, often called a comic strip.* The best known of printed joke forms today, but usually produced

My Favorite *Witticisms* Checklist

1 ☐	24 ☐	47 ☐	70 ☐	93 ☐	116 ☐
2 ☐	25 ☐	48 ☐	71 ☐	94 ☐	117 ☐
3 ☐	26 ☐	49 ☐	72 ☐	95 ☐	118 ☐
4 ☐	27 ☐	50 ☐	73 ☐	96 ☐	119 ☐
5 ☐	28 ☐	51 ☐	74 ☐	97 ☐	120 ☐
6 ☐	29 ☐	52 ☐	75 ☐	98 ☐	121 ☐
7 ☐	30 ☐	53 ☐	76 ☐	99 ☐	122 ☐
8 ☐	31 ☐	54 ☐	77 ☐	100 ☐	123 ☐
9 ☐	32 ☐	55 ☐	78 ☐	101 ☐	124 ☐
10 ☐	33 ☐	56 ☐	79 ☐	102 ☐	125 ☐
11 ☐	34 ☐	57 ☐	80 ☐	103 ☐	126 ☐
12 ☐	35 ☐	58 ☐	81 ☐	104 ☐	127 ☐
13 ☐	36 ☐	59 ☐	82 ☐	105 ☐	128 ☐
14 ☐	37 ☐	60 ☐	83 ☐	106 ☐	129 ☐
15 ☐	38 ☐	61 ☐	84 ☐	107 ☐	130 ☐
16 ☐	39 ☐	62 ☐	85 ☐	108 ☐	131 ☐
17 ☐	40 ☐	63 ☐	86 ☐	109 ☐	132 ☐
18 ☐	41 ☐	64 ☐	87 ☐	110 ☐	133 ☐
19 ☐	42 ☐	65 ☐	88 ☐	111 ☐	134 ☐
20 ☐	43 ☐	66 ☐	89 ☐	112 ☐	135 ☐
21 ☐	44 ☐	67 ☐	90 ☐	113 ☐	136 ☐
22 ☐	45 ☐	68 ☐	91 ☐	114 ☐	137 ☐
23 ☐	46 ☐	69 ☐	92 ☐	115 ☐	138 ☐
					139 ☐

See pp. 54–59 for ideas on collecting your own jokes.

139

A diplomat is a person who can tell you to go to hell in such a way that you actually look forward to the trip.

                                    Caskie Stinnett.

136

Since the earth's surface is ¼ land and ¾ water, it's obvious that we were intended to spend ¾ of our time fishing.

137

Pardon my bluntness but would you mind standing downwind.

138

"I've tried relaxing but—I don't know—I feel more comfortable, tense."
Hamilton Cartoon caption.

133

The Prime Minister of Israel, in declining a Burmese gift of an elephant, said that his rule was never to accept a gift that eats.

134

A decision is what a man makes when he can't find anyone to serve on a committee.

135

When Mrs. Glinski asked her husband if he would help straighten up the house, he replied: "Why? Is it tilted?"

130

If something can't go on forever, it will end.

131

A diplomat is one who thinks twice before he says nothing.

132

Harry Truman was Nancy Reagan's favorite piano player. Just the other night I thought she had on one of his records. It turned out to be a spoon that was caught in the garbage disposal.

128

A mother, worried over the possible wear and tear on the family nerves from her son's first musical efforts, asked Sir Thomas Beecham which instrument he should take up, the violin or the trombone. He recommended bagpipes, saying that they sound the same when you have mastered them as when you first begin. (Sir Thomas was the famed British conductor.)

129

When a husband said he couldn't think of anything to say to his mother-in-law, his wife replied: "Don't gimme that; there are hundreds of things you could apologize for."

120

Minnesota: where the elite meet the sleet.

121

A man who was considering joining a church, upon his arrival at the service, heard the minister reading from the Apostle Paul: "We have left undone those things we ought to have done and done those things we ought not to have done" and commented to the minister gratefully, as he was leaving the church: "At last, I have found my kind of people."

118

Robert Benchley book: "Success with Small Fruits." College courses he studied: "History of Lace Making," "Russian Taxation Systems before Catherine the Great," "North American Glacial Deposits," and "Early Renaissance Etchers." He became a very successful author.

119

Consistency requires you to be as ignorant today as you were a year ago. Bernard Berman.

116

An old timer reported that, in his barn-storming days, he used to drop his sister's Long Island paper to her from his plane. He said that if he tried that today in one of the modern planes, the paper would probably land in England.

117

When Will Rogers was in Europe, he said he didn't visit Queen Marie of Romania because he couldn't find the country.

114

Will Rogers proposed to solve the U Boat menace during World War I by boiling the ocean. When asked how to do that, he replied: "That's your problem; I'm just the idea man."

115

A man in a balloon is lost, hollers down to a man on the ground: "Where are we?" Man on the ground replies: "You are in a balloon." The balloonist says to his companion: "That must be a lawyer. He speaks with authority, talks directly to the point, and conveys no information."

111

"Progress might have been alright once but it has gone on too long."
>Ogden Nash.

112

W.C. Fields: "I am free of all prejudice. I hate everybody equally."

113

Groucho Marx: "Military intelligence is a contradiction in terms."

108

Christmas is the season when a lot of people come unglued trying to wrap things up.

109

W.C. Fields: "Women are like elephants to me: I like to look at them but I wouldn't want to own one."

110

Meditation: "It's not what you think."

105

While a farmer went overseas with the army, his girlfriend met another boyfriend, so she wrote the farmer a John Deere letter.

106

Kirk Douglas, while in Norway making a movie, asked a young man if it ever stopped raining. The young man's reply: "I don't know, I'm only 18."

107

A Hollywood mogul has built a new house that's in 4 area codes.

102

Cabbage: a vegetable about as large and wise as a man's head.

103

Charles Kraft: "Thanks to the Interstate Highway System it is now possible to travel from coast to coast without seeing anything."

104

A man, in seeking admission for his son, told the Dean that his son was a follower who got along well with others. The Dean replied: "Send him along; we already have 988 leaders and we need one follower."

98

What this country needs is a man who can be right and President at the same time.

99

The trouble with opera is that there's too much singing.

100

A closed mouth gathers no foot.

101

"Never eat more than you can lift."
Miss Piggy.

Meet Henry's Namesake

Henry W. Haverstock has been a practicing attorney and real estate investor for over forty-five years. As a teenager he contracted polio, which led to paralysis and many years of recovery. He was the first regular patient in the United States of Sister Kenny, the renowned Australian nurse. He was able to learn to walk with crutches, and has kept a keen sense of humor that he has used continually.

Haverstock graduated from the University of Minnesota in 1945, and received a law degree from the University of Southern California. He helped create a radio show, "You and the Law," which he emceed; and he is a life member of Courage Center, Golden Valley, Minnesota.

He lives in a Minneapolis suburb with his wife Shirley, and presents one-liners to Rotary, Kiwanis, YMCA, Exchange, Optimist, and Lions Clubs. He inspires everyone with direct talk and laughter. Many of the letters he regularly writes to editors of American newspapers have been published and are the basis for a future book.

88

A very self-important dowager: "My ancestors did not come over on the Mayflower; they had their own boat!"

89

A sign observed in a factory: "Firings will continue until morale improves."

90

A political war is where everybody shoots from the lip.

91

An actor said that his memory was perfect now, ever since he took the Sam Carnegie course.

92

Anything with a handle means work.

93

Phyllis Diller willed her body to science but science is contesting the Will.

94

A mummy is an Egyptian who has been pressed for time.

95

Minister: "You must pay for your sins. If you have already paid, you can ignore this notice."

96

You know the old proverb: A barking dog never bites. Yes, you know the proverb and I know the proverb but the question is, does the dog know the proverb?

97

A sharp nose indicates curiosity.
A flattened nose indicates too much curiosity.

Henry W. Haverstock, author of the most humorous and successful HENRY'S HILARIOUS ONELINERS, the first of a series of Henry's fun books. PHOTO CREDIT: ILGA CIMBULIS

85

Ross MacDonald: "There's nothing wrong with Southern California that a rise in the ocean level wouldn't cure."

86

Father to son: "You've got to set a goal and never quit. Remember George Washington?" "Yes" "Abraham Lincoln?" "Yes" "Azador McIngle?" "No, who was he?" Father: "See, you don't remember him. He quit."

87

Louis Brandeis: "Sunlight is the best of all disinfectants."

81

Will Rogers: "Live your life so that whenever you lose, you are ahead."

82

Ben Franklin: "Fish and visitors smell after 3 days."

83

G.B. Shaw: "If all the economists were laid end to end, they still would not reach a conclusion."

84

She runs the gamut of emotions, all the way from A to B.   Dorothy Parker.

77

Christopher Fry: "What, after all, is a halo? It's only one more thing to keep clean."

78

God save us from a bad neighbor and from a beginner on the trombone.

79

To err is human but it feels divine.

80

Definition of a gentleman farmer: One who has more hay in the bank than in the barn.

74

If you feel awed by people you encounter, just visualize them as being dressed in red woolen underwear.

75

People who think they know it all really annoy those of us who do.

76

A friend is someone who dislikes the same people you do.

71

Philosopher: "You should never finish something you haven't started."

72

There are three classes of people in the world: Those who make things happen, those who watch things happen and those who wonder what happened.

73

George Will: "An earthquake is a tough teacher but it tells the truth."

69

Typical question of student in 1965:
"What's the capitol of Wyoming?"
In 1975: "Where's Wyoming?"
In 1985: "Where is the United States?"
In 1995: "What planet are we on?"

70

Will Rogers said, in addressing a group of farmers: "Farmers, I am proud to report that the country as a whole is prosperous. I don't mean by that that the whole country is prosperous, but as a hole it is prosperous. That is, it is prosperous as a hole. A hole is not supposed to be prosperous and you are certainly in a hole."

66

Teacher: "Who was sorry when the prodigal son returned home?"
Student: "The fatted calf."

67

George Fisher: "When you aim for perfection, you discover that it's a moving target."

68

One good turn gets most of the blanket.

62

Square meals make round people.

63

A stock market rally is where you have lost your shirt and you get back a sleeve.

64

Is your husband a book worm? No, just an ordinary one.

65

Ben Franklin: "To find out a girl's faults, praise her to her girlfriends."

58

Mark Twain: "He had no principles and was delightful company."

59

Today is the tomorrow you worried about yesterday.

60

Love your enemies in case your friends turn out to be a bunch of bastards.

61

A murderer is one who is presumed innocent until he is proven insane.

54

If it wasn't for half of the people in the world, the other half would be all of them.

55

One psychiatrist advertises: "A cure guaranteed or your mania back."

56

The hardest thing to learn is which bridge to burn and which to cross.

57

You can't make footprints in the sands of time sitting down.

50

If your wife wants to learn to drive, don't stand in her way.

51

Rural life is found mostly in the country.

52

He's not a bad guy until you get to know him.

53

Doctor, I demand a second opinion.
"Okay, I'll tell you again."

46

A pessimist is one who feels bad when he feels good for fear he'll feel worse when he feels better.

47

Early to bed and early to rise, and you'll meet very few of our best people.

48

He died at twenty but was buried at seventy.

49

Defeat isn't bitter if you don't swallow it.

43

Sign on a plumber's window: "Do it yourself. Then call us before it's too late."

44

My problem is that it takes me six weeks to read the book of the month.

45

Napoleon: "Religion is what keeps the poor people from murdering the rich."

40

There are two kinds of people: Those who don't know and those who don't know that they don't know.

41

W.C. Fields: "Start every day with a smile and get it over with."

42

J. Paul Getty: "The meek shall inherit the earth—but not the mineral rights."

36

A reformer is a guy who rides through a sewer in a glass bottomed boat.

37

Nobody ever bets enough on a winning horse.

38

Most of our future lies ahead.

39

"What this country needs is more unemployed politicians." Edward Langley.

33

The United Nations keeps the peace. In forty years, there has never been a war in the UN building.

34

My wife ran off with my best friend and I miss him, too.

35

Yogi Berra was asked if he wanted his pizza in eight or twelve pieces. His answer: "You better make it eight; I don't think I could eat twelve pieces."

30

"Do your boats sink often?" Answer: "Only once."

31

Kermit the frog: "It isn't easy being green."

32

Truman: "I never did give anybody hell. I just told the truth and they thought it was hell."

26

The world is proof that God is a committee.   Bob Stokes.

27

A man is as young as the woman he feels.

28

The child had every toy that his father ever wanted.

29

Wherever you go, there you are.

23

"We must believe in luck; for how else can we explain the success of those we don't like?"   Jean Cocteau.

24

The more he talked of his honor, the faster we counted our spoons.
Ralph Waldo Emerson.

25

If you put dirty things on paper, you can get sued unless you're a parakeet.

19

Don't worry about flying. It's not dangerous. Crashing is dangerous.

20

Faith is believing what you know ain't so.   Mark Twain.

21

The less things change, the more they stay the same.

22

Schizophrenia beats eating alone.

15

Joggers and jogging are not to be sniffed at.

16

Scoreboard at a Roman coliseum:
Lions 21, Christians 6.

17

Have you heard about the tree surgeon who fell out of his patient?

18

I have a friend who drowned while taking acupuncture on a waterbed.

11

In our society, a man is known by the company he owns.

12

How to save on defense: Use last year's rockets but add new grills.

13

Is that all there is to the story? Yes, I've already told you more than I heard.

14

I hate intolerant people.

7

A government bureau is where the taxpayer's shirt is kept.

8

A diplomat is a man who knows how far he can go before he has gone too far.

9

W.C. Fields: "They had a butler who drank too much—sort of an old family container."

10

Hell hath no fury like the lawyer of a woman scorned.

4

Did you hear about John? He bought a Louis XIV bed but it was too small for him so he sent it back and ordered a Louis XV.

5

Teacher to student: "What was the former Russian leader called?" Tsar. "His wife?" Tsarina. "His children?" Tsardines.

6

"Why did you get drunk in the first place?" "I didn't get drunk in the first place. I got drunk in the last place."

1

A sensible girl is not so sensible as she looks because a sensible girl has more sense than to look sensible.

2

Mae West: "Too much of a good thing can be wonderful."

3

Alexander Graham Bell Polaski was the first telephone pole.

I am happy to report that they usually bring a good laugh, though sometimes only a good natured groan—or, on rare occasion, hisses or boos.

Very little of my humor is original but much of it has undergone re-wording. This is due in large part to my inability to write as fast as the stories are told oratorically. With the printed word, this has not, of course, presented the same problem.

In any case, it will be for you, the reader, to determine whether my choice of one-liners produces for you, health-giving laughter. Since one-liners are short and generally easy to remember, I hope that you can use some of them to add interest and sparkle to all of your own social encounters.

Have fun.

Henry W. Haverstock
Minneapolis
March, 1992

Dedication
To All Those People Who Love To Laugh

Introduction
Laughter is good for the spirit. Laughter promotes good health. The late Norman Cousins, in his book *Anatomy of an Illness*, showed how laughter in his own life helped him survive a near-fatal disability and extended his life for many years.

Increasingly, laughter is recognized as an essential element to a balanced life. In recognition of this, a new TV channel was recently set up for cable TV, devoted exclusively to funny, laugh-producing programming.

For many years—and without any particular system about it—I have enjoyed collecting what I considered funny one-liners. Some time ago, I decided to bring these random bits and pieces together. At the same time, I have been testing these one-liners before various groups in which I am active, including Rotary, Exchange Clubs, and the Y's Men's clubs.

Ladies and Gentlemen, Children of All Ages...

Welcome to fun and humor by my close friend and associate, and namesake, Henry my man.

As The One and Only LAUGHING MOUSE, I, Henry of Hopkins, seek nothing more than for you to be joyful and happy. And from time to time when you find it in your heart to leave a little cheese around, I would be most appreciative.

The material contained in this book has been collected over many years from a variety of sources, often passed on to me by my associates, to be used in my various talks before clubs and business dinners. Many of the original authors are unknown, and some one-liners have been attributed to more than one author. Therefore, it is truly impossible to list each source. I would like for this to be an acknowledgment of appreciation to the authors for the thoughts, if not the words, of witticism contained herein.   *Henry W. Haverstock*